WILD FOOD FROM LAND AND SEA

Marco Pierre White

EBURY PRESS

LONDON

For Mati:
also for my daughter Leticia, my son Luciano,
and the grandmother they never knew.

First published in 1994

This edition published in 1996 by
Ebury Press, Random House, 20 Vauxhall Bridge Road,
London SW1V 2SA

1 3 5 7 9 10 8 6 4 2

Text copyright © Marco Pierre White 1994

Random House Australia Pty Limited, 20 Alfred Street, Milsons Point,
Sydney, New South Wales 2061, Australia

Random House New Zealand Limited, 18 Poland Road, Glenfield,
Auckland 10, New Zealand

Random House South Africa Pty Limited, PO Box 337, Bergvlei,
South Africa

Random House UK Limited Reg. No. 95400

A CIP catalogue record for this book is available from the British Library.

ISBN 0 09 181415 4

Designed by The Senate and Bob Vickers

Printed and bound in Great Britain by
Mackays of Chatham plc, Kent

Marco Pierre White learned his skills as the protégé of Albert Roux at the famous Gavroche restaurant, before opening his own, Harvey's in Wandsworth, south-west London, in 1987. At 25 years old he became the youngest chef ever to win two Michelin stars for Harvey's. In 1992 he opened The Canteen, and in 1993 his latest venture, The Restaurant in the Hyde Park Hotel, was launched and immediately gained two Michelin stars. He is now the only restaurateur in Britain to have two restaurants with these coveted awards. His previous book, *White Heat*, was published in 1990.

CONTENTS

INTRODUCTION

Six years ago my first cookery book, *White Heat*, was published. Since then I've left one restaurant and have started three more, I've gained three stars and a son, and I think I've calmed down somewhat!

My cooking has probably mellowed too, and this second book of recipes reflects this. It actually amazes me sometimes that people want to buy cookery books written by chefs, because there is such a gulf between what we do in the professional kitchen and what can be done at home. No domestic cook can ever achieve what we can because they lack the hands, the time, the facilities, the finance – so they're starting 50 yards behind. But people still seem to want to know what goes on behind the swing doors of our kitchens, they still want to know our 'secrets'.

What we are giving in our cookery books is a distillation of knowledge. No one buying this or any other chef's book is going to become a great cook overnight. They need to learn the craft of cooking, the basic essentials, before they can start to be really creative. Once that foundation has been established, then they can start to build on it. There's nothing really all that new in cooking – you can't re-invent the wheel, after all – but once you know your onions, so to speak, you can create away to your heart's content. It's enlightening to look back at some of my early menus at Harvey's, for instance; there are some very simple combinations there, classics, which I obviously relied on while I was perfecting my craft.

What someone buying this book will get, though, are a few of the ideas and concepts I have learned, created, borrowed or adapted during those years of acquiring knowledge. There are the old favourites here, which appear in almost every cookery book – the stocks without which a sauce would not taste right, and the sauces which are the making of any dish, whether simple or elaborate. There are also some more creative ideas, combinations which have worked well for me, and which I hope will do the same for you.

People should use recipes as a guideline only (which I'm sure most do anyway). Timings can vary considerably, depending on ovens, pans, cuts of meat or whatever. The way I present things – with a cornucopia of garnishes – may not be so easy in the domestic kitchen, but I'm only recording what *we* do. If you want to do something different, you are of course perfectly free to do so (which is why I've got a whole section of basic recipes which, in many cases, are virtually interchangeable). Two or three garnishes may be putting you under too much pressure, so cut it down to one. So long as the main element of the dish – the meat or fish – is perfectly cooked, it should all work. For instance, you might like to roast your normal cut of beef in your usual way, but accompany it with a wonderful red wine sauce from the book instead of a gravy. If it is easier for you to poach a whole salmon instead of cutting it into escalopes or steaks, do so; served with my hollandaise, nothing could be more delicious. By making a mayonnaise to accompany a crab, and doing that well, you're already on the right road.

You could forget all the extraneous detail in individual recipes, and just serve a piece of perfectly cooked red mullet with a sauce vierge. You don't even have to take the fish off the bone, but could grill it whole on the barbecue and serve a pot of the sauce at the side. It's a case of creative thinking, and by taking it slowly, adapting and borrowing from individual recipes, you'll get lots of ideas, lots of practice, and will, I hope, find it all interesting and enlightening.

None of the recipes here are, in essence, very difficult. Very few restaurant recipes are, really. What makes restaurant dishes look impressive, and makes some domestic cooks think they're beyond their scope, is what we do with them, how we present them, and how we put it all together in different concepts and combinations. One element in the book may help you in this respect. Many of the basic recipes – for sauces or for accompanying vegetables or garnishes – can be made in advance and chilled or frozen. With those out of the way, so to speak, you can then concentrate on the parts of the dish that need to be achieved at the last minute. Similarly, I've presented a few recipes as we would approach them in the restaurant kitchen, with instructions on how to cook a dish for one person only. This has a sort of dual purpose: there are a lot of single people out there who are put off by recipes for four or six; and I also think it highlights what is actually happening behind those swing doors. As I said, I can be grilling a perfect piece of fish, while someone else is doing the potatoes, yet another the sauce and the garnish. At home this could be less easy, but it's not entirely insurmountable. And to serve for more than one, simply multiply the quantities.

In France, because of the different food ethos or culture, the great chefs can get away with offering a simple roast chicken, grilled sea bream with a red wine sauce, or salmon with a sorrel sauce. That cutting right through to the essentials is something I'd like to do as well, but nine out of ten of my customers wouldn't understand it. There is a different mentality in Britain, and thus I have to give them more to look at on the plate, and more to actually eat. Because gastronomy is an industry in France, French chefs can present food much more simply than we can here. I'd prefer not to serve anything with my salmon and tapenade, for instance, but I'm in a service industry and, to a certain extent, what the customer wants and expects, I have to respect. Chefs should not really be telling people how to eat. We've got to compromise to be commercial.

A young female food writer recently asked why chefs couldn't cook a nice plain piece of grilled fish. Well, we can and we do, but we have to dress it up for our customers. No one would be happy to pay up to £60 per head for something that could easily be cooked at home. People come to restaurants like mine for precisely the foods and dishes they can't easily get in their local shops, or are reluctant to cook themselves – like lobster, langoustines, foie gras. There's absolutely nothing wrong with a nice piece of grilled fish, but most diners want something more exciting when they're out to have a good time.

That's what I dislike about food critics, whether in magazines, newspapers or food guides, this lack of true insight into what we do, their blinkered attitude. Very few of them have undergone the long, exhaustive and exhausting years of training we have, yet they feel licensed to pontificate about restaurants, food, chefs and their cooking, sometimes destroying a hard-won reputation overnight. Far too often their reviews reveal to us chefs just how *little* they actually know about food.

There are only a handful of critics whose opinions I respect – they have been around a long time, they have eaten in enough establishments, and are good cooks themselves. But sadly there are many more who lack style (would you come to a two-star restaurant wearing a cricket sweater, or bicycle clips?), who lack knowledge (one revered critic's last job was on the sports pages!), who are envious of others' success, and who are therefore lacking considerably in good judgement. I think it totally irrelevant to criticise the decor of a restaurant – all such things are personal, and what does it matter anyway? – or to elaborate for half the review on the designer clothing worn by the restaurant's clientele, male and female. Eating out *can* be an all-round experience, encompassing surroundings and fellow eaters, but it's the food that matters ultimately. When they home in on all these other things, it really makes me wonder if they can write *at all* about food. And in all honesty, I don't think someone who runs sausage-cooking competitions in a newspaper should be allowed within a mile of a top-class restaurant . . .

And their methods of judging chefs and restaurants are, I think, little short of immoral on occasion. A top chef can be hauled over the coals because of one less than totally successful dish, because of, say, a wait of a little longer than expected, or for cold bread. Nick Faldo doesn't hit the green every time, Bjorn Borg didn't serve an ace every service game, Sebastian Coe didn't win gold every time he ran, so *we* are allowed to get it wrong every now and again as well. No top chef is ever going to serve *bad* food, and it certainly could never be so bad that it's worthy of total condemnation. I have to admit that I think food critics in Britain should not, on the whole, be taken seriously.

The *Guide Michelin*, on the other hand, judges you entirely on what you put on the plate and on the service. They don't criticise anybody, they don't make facetious comments, they don't run people down, they don't tell people how to run their businesses, so it's a guide in the true meaning of the word. When I had long hair, when I was renowned for asking people to leave, when I had a bad press, Michelin were never influenced by that. (Most of my reputation is a product of exaggeration and ignorance anyway.)

I honestly think the most rewarding thing in my career has been the support I've had from Michelin. The French guide has been published every year since 1900; the British one has existed for much less long, but it's now *the* guide to the best restaurants and hotels in the country. Its ratings are regarded as the most objective and impartial, and its judgements are awaited in January every year with bated breath by all of us in the restaurant world.

The Michelin good food stars are awarded as follows:

A very good restaurant in its category ★

Excellent cooking, worth a detour ★★

Exceptional cuisine, worth a special journey ★★★

The other amenities – such as decor etc – are measured separately, with the crossed spoon and fork symbol, and range from 'plain but good' with one symbol, to 'luxury' with five.

Michelin make their awards on the basis of reports from a team of full-time inspectors, as well as letters from the public. The inspectors are recruited from the hotel and restaurant industry, and are highly knowledgeable about every aspect of management, as well as how every classic dish should be prepared. How many food critics can boast that sort of background, and that sort of expertise?

Every listed restaurant is re-checked annually, starred ones more often, and we never know when an inspector will call. He (or she) reserves a table like any member of the public, without revealing his purpose until after the bill is paid. He then explains who he is and asks to see the kitchen and cellar. He will report on all the things that any discriminating customer would look for – the quality of the food, the service, the ambience, the inventiveness of the dishes, the range of the wine list.

At the top level, promotions and demotions are very carefully considered – particularly demotions, since Michelin are well aware of the effect the removal of stars can have on a restaurant's business. I wish food critics would think similarly before letting fly with their unconsidered brickbats.

Many food critics in Britain are actually critical of Michelin. Maybe they object to a foreign tyre company wielding so much power over the restaurant business here, or to its perhaps old-fashioned insistence on continuity and maintaining the highest possible standards. This necessarily precludes them from judging or responding to the new fashions and trends of the moment – the latest restaurant to serve bastardised Italian or sagebrush chicken with sun-dried tomatillos. . . . I actually think that the food critics here are jealous of Michelin, of the credibility Michelin gets from chefs. The *Guide Michelin* is reliable, objective, and in my opinion has done more for gastronomy in this country than anything or anybody else.

I firmly believe that if it weren't for Michelin I wouldn't be where I am today, but other people's support has been vital as well. The food business is essentially a small one, we all know each other – there is a fraternity of chefs, if you like – and we all influence each other as well as compete with each other. Some become closer in friendship, some don't, but I've included here recipes given by those who are and have been closest to me. These are the people who have encouraged me, inspired me, contributed to my style and way of cooking, who have helped me and defended me over the years. They have shared in what I have achieved, and so I'm sharing their talents with you.

As they helped me in the past, so I'm now in the lucky position of being able to help others. A lot of people have accused me of an unlikely number of sins, including that I'm bad for the catering industry, but I *am* contributing, not least in furthering the cause of top-class English cooking. My kitchens are packed with potential talent, young *commis* and *sous* chefs whom I train, and who will one day take over their own restaurants and carry the message even further. It's very exciting for me to think of my kitchens as a 'nursery' for the future, just as those of chefs like Albert Roux or Raymond Blanc have been.

That's perhaps how one should look at this book too. If even one of my recipes inspires you to greater things, then my effort has paid off, and the price you paid for the book was worth it!

MARCO PIERRE WHITE

STARTER DISHES

Vichyssoise of Oyster, Caviar Chantilly

The fish stock can be made in advance and frozen, and the soup a few hours in advance.

Cook and add the oysters at the last moment.

---

4 portions

400 g (14 oz) leeks, finely sliced	salt and freshly ground white pepper
175 g (6 oz) onions, finely sliced	
50 g (2 oz) unsalted butter	Garnishes
175 g (6 oz) potatoes, sliced paper thin	12 oysters
	4 tablespoons *oscietra* caviar
450 ml (15 fl oz) Fish Stock (basic 7)	4 tablespoons whipped double cream
450 ml (15 fl oz) water	4 tablespoons chopped chives
100 ml (3½ fl oz) double cream	

---

1. Sweat together the leek and onion in the butter in a large pan without colouring. Add the potatoes.

2. Meanwhile bring the fish stock and water up to the boil. Add to the leek and onion pan, and cook rapidly for 8 minutes.

3. Add the cream and cook for a further 2 minutes.

4. Place in a processor or blender and pureé, then pass through a fine sieve. Season to taste.

5. Open the oysters, saving their juices. Pass the juices through a fine sieve into a small pan and poach the oysters in this for 30 seconds on each side. *Do not boil.*

6. Mix the caviar into the whipped cream.

7. Place three oysters in the bottom of each warm soup bowl, then cover with hot soup.

8. Sprinkle with chives, and then place a quenelle of Chantilly cream (the cream and caviar) on top.

Soup of Red Mullet with Saffron

Make the fish stock well in advance and freeze.

Start the soup the day before, by marinating the mullet.

4 portions

10 red mullet
100 ml (3¹/₂ fl oz) olive oil
1 pinch saffron strands
1 pinch cayenne pepper
1 onion
¹/₂ head of celery
¹/₂ fennel bulb
¹/₂ head of garlic
250 g (9 oz) fresh tomatoes
about 450 g (1 lb) tomato
  pureé

175 ml (6 fl oz) each of
  Pernod and Cognac
2 litres (3¹/₂ pints) Fish Stock
  (basic 7)
¹/₂ large potato, thinly sliced

Garnishes
Rouille 2 (basic 25)
Gruyère cheese, grated
small crisp croûtons

1. Scale the mullet, and cut off the heads. Remove and discard the innards, plus the gills and eyes. Wash all the pieces thoroughly in cold water. Cut the bodies up into three equal-sized pieces. Place, heads and all, in a dish.

2. Mix the oil with the saffron and cayenne, and add to the fish. Mix and leave to marinate in a cold place for 24 hours.

3. Peel and trim the onion, celery, fennel and garlic as appropriate. Cut into small dice (*mirepoix*). Dice the tomatoes.

4. Roast the vegetable *mirepoix* in a large saucepan in a little of the marinade oil until golden. Add the tomato dice and when the tomato liquid has disappeared, add the tomato pureé. Cook slowly for about 10 minutes.

5. Meanwhile, remove the mullet pieces from their marinade and pan-fry separately until golden brown, a few minutes on each side.

6. Pour the Pernod and Cognac into the *mirepoix* pan and set alight. Reduce over heat until the alcohol has cooked out, then add the mullet.

7. Cover the fish and vegetables with the fish stock, adding some water if necessary. Add the potato and simmer for 1¹/₂ hours.

8. Blend in a food processor, bones and all, then pass through a fine sieve – up to six times for the finest texture.

9. Serve in hot soup plates, with bowls of rouille, grated Gruyère and croûtons offered separately.

Pistou de Saint-Jacques

The soup base – the vegetables and stock etc – can be prepared in advance, and reheated briefly at the last moment.

The pistou can be made in advance and chilled.

Do not add the pistou or scallops until the very end.

---

6 portions

30 g (1¼ oz) each of prepared and finely diced onion, carrot, celeriac, turnip, swede, potato, green beans and courgette
olive oil
1 litre (1¾ pints) Clam, Mussel and Fish Stock (basic 8)

salt and freshly ground white pepper

Garnishes
6 scallops, shelled and cleaned
Court Bouillon to cover (basic 10)
100 g (4 oz) spaghetti
6 tablespoons Pistou (basic 35)

---

1. Sweat the onion in a little olive oil in a saucepan then add the carrot and celeriac. After a few minutes add the turnip, swede and potato, and sweat for a few minutes more. Add the beans and courgettes at the very end.
2. Bring the stock to the boil in a separate pan and pour over the vegetables. Bring back to the boil, then remove from the heat and season to taste.
3. Meanwhile, wash the scallops briefly and pat dry. Cut the nuggets of white meat into three slices horizontally. Poach for 1 minute only in the court bouillon with a little olive oil added. Drain.
4. Break the spaghetti into 2.5 cm (1 in) lengths, and blanch separately in boiling salted water. Drain well and add to the vegetable soup.
5. To finish, divide the hot soup between the hot soup plates, and add 1 tablespoon pistou to each. Stir to emulsify, then pop three slices of poached scallop into each.

Cappuccino of Mushrooms with Crayfish Tails and Chervil

The soup can be made a day in advance.

6 portions

1 kg (2¼ lb) very white mushrooms, finely sliced
1 onion, sliced
1 white of leek, sliced
20 g (¾ oz) unsalted butter
100 g (4 oz) potatoes, sliced
1 litre (1¾ pints) Double Chicken Stock (basic 2)

1 litre (1¾ pints) double cream

Garnishes
18 crayfish tails
fresh chervil leaves

1. Sweat the mushrooms, onion and leek in the butter until most of the moisture in the vegetables has evaporated.
2. In a separate pan, simmer the potatoes in the chicken stock and cream until tender.
3. Bring the potatoes to the boil, pour over the mushrooms, and cook gently together for 10 minutes. Liquidise the whole lot and pass through a fine sieve.
4. Steam the crayfish tails for 1 minute. Place three in the bottom of each warmed soup plate.
5. Reheat the soup, trying not to boil it. Using a hand mixer, blend the soup to incorporate air and make it frothy.
6. Pour the hot soup into the plates on top of the crayfish tails and sprinkle with chervil.

Watercress Soup with Poached Egg

This simple soup can be made earlier in the day and reheated.

4 portions

100 g (4 oz) watercress
   leaves
1 litre (1¾ pints) water
25 g (1 oz) clarified butter

1 medium potato, peeled and
   very thinly sliced
salt
4 eggs, poached

1. Bring the water to the boil in a pan.

2. In a separate pan with a large surface area, heat the clarified butter until very hot.

3. Add the watercress leaves to the hot clarified butter and cook for 2 minutes.

4. Add the potato slices to the pan.

5. Add the boiling water to the watercress and potato, bring to the boil and cook for 2-3 minutes, or until the potato is just cooked.

6. Remove from the heat. Season lightly with salt, then liquidise and pass through a fine strainer.

7. Place a freshly poached egg in the bottom of each soup plate, and pour the hot soup over it.

Oysters with Scrambled Egg and Caviar

Make the sauce in advance.

---

1 portion

5 oysters, no. 2
50 ml (2 fl oz) Velouté for
   Fish (basic 14)
salt and freshly ground white
   pepper
lemon juice

15 g (¹/₂ oz) unsalted butter
2 eggs, beaten
1 teaspoon double cream
2 teaspoons caviar
sprigs of chervil

---

1. Open the oysters, saving their juices and their shells. Pass the juices through a fine sieve into a small pan. Clean the shells out and warm them (under the grill or in a low oven).

2. Poach the oysters in their juices in the pan, on both sides, for no more than 45 seconds altogether.

3. Bring the velouté to the boil to reduce it a little, then season with salt and a little lemon juice. Froth up with a little hand-mixer.

4. Melt the butter in another saucepan and quickly scramble the eggs, seasoning with salt and pepper. Remove from the heat and add the cream to stop the cooking.

5. Fill the warm oyster shells with scrambled eggs, and place the oysters on top. Cover with the sauce and garnish with the caviar and chervil.

> **TIP**
>
> *You could of course simply serve the oysters and scrambled eggs on a plate instead of in the shells. You could also flavour the sauce at the last moment with snipped chives.*

Salad of Lobster with New Potatoes and Truffle

Start this salad the day before, so the potatoes will have a chance to marinate properly.

The stocks and vinaigrette can be made well in advance.

---

1 portion

Court Bouillon to cover
  (basic 10)
1 x 450 g (1 lb) lobster
salt and freshly ground white
  pepper

Garnishes
6 new potatoes
Chicken Stock to cover
  (basic 1)
about 150 ml (5 fl oz)
  Vinaigrette 1 (basic 29)
8 thin slices black truffle
sea salt flakes (*fleur de sel*)
fresh chervil leaves

---

1. Scrape the new potatoes, then cook them in the stock until tender. Pour off the stock, and replace with enough of the vinaigrette to just cover. Leave to marinate overnight in a cool place, turning occasionally.

2. Bring the court bouillon to the boil. Drop in the lobster then take off the heat. Leave the fish in the liquid for 30 minutes. Drain well.

3. Slice the potatoes into thin discs and arrange to cover the bottom of the plate. Warm the plate briefly under the preheated grill.

4. Remove the lobster flesh from the shell, and slice it into medallions. Arrange these on top of the potatoes.

5. Garnish the lobster with the black truffle slices, and sprinkle the plate with a little vinaigrette, *fleur de sel* and the chervil.

Tian of Crab and Tomato

Make the sauces in advance, but the assembly has to be fairly last-minute.

There is a certain amount of wastage on this dish.

---

4 portions

225 g (8 oz) white crab meat
20 large, even-sized red
    Dutch tomatoes, blanched
    and skinned
1 round lettuce
1 bunch watercress
about 25 ml (1 fl oz)
    Vinaigrette 2 (basic 30)
2 Golden Delicious apples

1 avocado
juice of 1 lemon
3 tablespoons Mayonnaise
    (basic 23)

Garnishes
120 ml (4 fl oz) Tomato
    Coulis (basic 33)
8 chervil leaves

---

1. Cut a thin slice off the stem end of each tomato, then place cut side down on the work surface. Cut a slice off at each side of the tomato. Scoop out all the flesh and seeds, and 'unroll' the tomato so that it forms a rectangle. You should have twenty rectangles, which form the layers of the tian.

2. Cut the lettuce and watercress leaves into fine ribbons (*chiffonade*). Keep separate, and dress both with a little vinaigrette.

3. Peel and core the apples, and cut into 3 mm (1/8 in) dice. Peel, stone and dice the avocado similarly. Keep separate, but sprinkle both with lemon juice to prevent oxidation.

4. Shred the crab meat and mix with the mayonnaise and shredded lettuce.

5. Mix the watercress, apple and avocado together.

6. Lay the tomato slices on a board side by side, four per portion. On the bottom one, place a little of the lettuce and crab. Top with another tomato rectangle and cover with more lettuce and crab. Top with yet another tomato rectangle and cover with some of the watercress, apple and avocado mixture. Top each tian with the final layer of tomato.

7. Using a very sharp knife, cut down at an angle on both ends of the layered rectangle, transforming it into a diamond shape.

8. Place a small amount of tomato coulis in the middle of each plate. Place the tomato tian in the centre, then garnish with a chervil leaf at each end.

TIP

The fillings for the tian can vary, and you could also decorate the coulis with dots of green mayonnaise. The tian could also be cut into a circle, using a very sharp cutter.

Roast Sea Scallops, Sauce Vierge

Everything must be done at the last moment.

1 portion

2 fresh, large scallops	Garnishes
salt and freshly ground white pepper	2 tablespoons Sauce Vierge (basic 26)
1 teaspoon olive oil	a few fresh herbs (tarragon, chives, chervil)

1. Wash the scallops in cold water quickly, dry and refrigerate for at least 30 minutes.
2. When the scallops are firm, remove from the fridge and slice each of them in half. Season with a little salt.
3. Make the sauce, adding the tomato dice as you serve.
4. In a frying pan heat the olive oil. Sauté the scallop slices in the hot oil, turning each side when golden brown, cooking until medium rare, about 2 minutes in all.
5. Pour the sauce on to the plate, and arrange the slices of scallop on top. Garnish with the herbs.

Sea Scallops with Lemon and Cinnamon

Make the stock and pastry well in advance.

Keep the skirt and trimmings in the freezer to contribute to your *next* scallop stock.

1 portion

2 large scallops, shelled and cleaned (keep the skirts and trimmings)	a tiny piece of cinnamon stick, crushed
a little white wine vinegar	a little grated lemon zest
1 celery stalk	100 ml (3¹/₂ fl oz) Scallop Stock (basic 8)
¹/₂ carrot	20 g (³/₄ oz) Puff Pastry (basic 66)
¹/₂ shallot	1 egg, beaten
20 g (³/₄ oz) unsalted butter	
salt and freshly ground white pepper	

1. Pat the scallop flesh dry and place in the fridge to 'set'.

2. Take one of the shells, both top and bottom, and clean thoroughly. Boil for 3 minutes in water with a little vinegar to sterilise. Remove from the water, dry and leave to get cold.

3. Cut half the celery and carrot into long *julienne* strips. Chop the shallot finely.

4. Sweat the celery and carrot *julienne* in 1 teaspoon of the butter for a few minutes, then season with salt and pepper. Drain and reserve.

5. Place the vegetable *julienne* in the bottom half of the sterilised scallop shell. Cut the scallops in half and place on top. Sprinkle with the cinnamon and lemon zest. Cover with stock and place the top shell on.

6. Roll the pastry out and cut into a thin strip long and wide enough to seal the scallop shell join (about 30 x 3.75 cm/ 12 x 1½ in). Egg wash the edges of the shell, and seal with the pastry.

7. Bake the sealed scallop in the oven well preheated to 240°C/475°F/Gas 9, for 10-12 minutes, or until the pastry is golden brown.

8. Bring out of the oven and crack open with a knife. Remove the top shell. Carefully pour the stock into a small pan. Bring to the boil, then melt in the remaining butter. Pour back over the scallops and vegetables in the shell.

Risotto of Ink with Roast Calamares

Prepare the risotto base a couple of hours in advance; finish at the last minute.

2 portions

2 small squid, cleaned
50 ml (2 fl oz) olive oil
25 ml (1 fl oz) white wine
1 tablespoon chopped
   parsley

salt and freshly ground white
   pepper

Garnish
Risotto of Ink (basics 38, 40)

1. Have ready the basic risotto, and transform into an ink risotto not long before serving.

2. Cut the squid flesh into narrow strips.

3. Cook the strips in the hot olive oil to seal, but not colour.

4. Deglaze the pan with the white wine, stirring, then bring to the boil. Add the chopped parsley and seasoning to taste.

5. Add to the finished risotto.

TIP

The risotto base (basic 38) can be prepared in advance and kept in the fridge for up to 4 hours until you are ready to make Risotto of Ink (basic 40) for this recipe.

Ravioli of Langoustine, Sauce Albufera

Make the pasta well in advance.
   Prepare the ravioli beforehand, as well as the sauce.

4 portions

1 quantity Fresh Pasta (basic 65)	1 egg yolk
20 langoustines, nos 1 or 2	Garnishes
salt and freshly ground white pepper	**Sauce Albufera (basic 13)**
10 g (¼ oz) black truffle, very finely chopped	**Buttered Cabbage (basic 47)**

1. Roll the pasta out to 1 mm thick. Cut into twenty 10 cm (4 in) squares. Place on cling film on a plate, cover with cling film, and store in the fridge to rest.

2. Blanch the langoustines in boiling water, about 1½-2 minutes, then shell when cool enough to handle. Dry well and season the tails with salt and pepper. (Keep the shells and freeze for stocks, sauces etc.)

3. Arrange the squares of pasta in front of you, cling film removed. Place a langoustine tail in the centre of each, and sprinkle with some of the truffle.

4. Mix the egg yolk, then brush over the edges of the pasta. Fold the pasta around the langoustines, making sure there is no air trapped, and that the edges will hold well together. Trim with scissors, emphasising the natural half-moon-like shape.

5. Poach the ravioli in boiling salted water for 4 minutes. Drain well.

6. Warm the sauce, and cook the cabbage at the last moment.

7. Place five ravioli on each warm plate, and coat with the sauce. Garnish with a mound of bright green cabbage.

Tagliatelle aux Ecrevisses du Windrush

Raymond Blanc, Le Manoir aux Quat' Saisons, Oxfordshire

In many ways Raymond changed my views about cooking. He did as much as anyone for me, if not more, in my life as a cook. I would be delighted to see him get his third Michelin star because I know just how much he's put into his hotel and restaurant.

---

4 portions

24 large freshwater crayfish
salt and freshly ground white
   pepper
1 tablespoon clarified butter
200 g (7 oz) tagliatelle
   (uncooked weight)
20 g (³/₄ oz) unsalted butter

For the sauce
30 g (1¹/₄ oz) unsalted
   butter
30 g (1¹/₄ oz) each of
   carrots, leeks, celery and
   shallots, prepared as
   appropriate and diced

1 garlic clove, crushed
8 tarragon leaves
1 sprig fresh thyme
2 tomatoes, seeded and
   chopped
20 g (³/₄ oz) clarified butter
50 ml (2 fl oz) Cognac
200 ml (7 fl oz) dry white
   wine, reduced by
   one-third
250-300 ml (8-10 fl oz) cold
   water
1 tablespoon whipping
   cream

---

1. *Preparing the crayfish* This recipe is not for the faint-hearted, as freshwater crayfish have got many means of self-defence!

You need to separate the body from the head and claws, and the most humane way of doing this is to kill the crayfish by piercing its head with the point of a sharp knife. Twist the body from the head and detach the tail. Pinch the middle part of the tail, twist and pull to remove the intestine. Separate the claws from the legs. Reserve with the tails. Cut the heads length-ways, and remove and discard the stomach and intestines.

Reserve the heads for the sauce.

2. *Making the sauce* In a small casserole, melt 10 g (¼ oz) of the butter and gently sweat the diced vegetables, along with the garlic and herbs, for 10 minutes. Add the tomatoes after 5 minutes.

In a separate, larger, casserole, heat the clarified butter to very hot, and sear the heads of the crayfish until they turn scarlet. Spoon out the fat, add the Cognac and boil for 1 second. Add the contents of the first casserole, and then add the reduced white wine. Barely cover with water, bring to the boil, skim and simmer for 15 minutes.

Purée the head shells and the stock in the liquidiser, then strain through a fine chinois sieve, then through a muslin cloth.

On a brisk heat, reduce these juices down to 150 ml (5 fl oz). Add the cream and whisk in the remaining 20 g (¾ oz) butter, very cold and cut into dice. Taste, and season first with salt, then pepper and finally a further dash of Cognac if necessary.

3. *Cooking the crayfish tails and claws* Blanch the tails and claws in boiling salted water for 10 seconds. Drain. Remove the shells from both claws and tails, taking great care not to damage the claws. Finish cooking the tails and claws by sautéing in the clarified butter for 1 minute only. Taste and season with salt and pepper. Reserve.

4. *Cooking the tagliatelle* Bring 2 litres (3½ pints) water to a fast boil with 30 g (1¼ oz) salt. Cook fresh tagliatelle for 2 minutes, dry for 3-5 minutes. Drain, stir in the butter, then season with salt and pepper.

5. *Serving* Arrange the pasta attractively in the middle of each plate. Reheat the sauce, spoon around the tagliatelle and arrange the tail and claw flesh on top.

Terrine of Foie Gras

Start this a couple of days in advance.

Use a terrine or pâté mould 40 cm (16 in) in length, and line it with four or five layers of cling film, leaving enough overlap to cover the top.

This makes the terrine easier to extract from the mould.

---

18 portions

8 x 800 g (1³/₄ lb) lobes of foie gras	**¹/₄ bottle Armagnac**
salt and freshly ground white pepper	Garnishes
¹/₂ bottle white port	**Madeira Jelly (basic 6)**
	toasted slices of brioche

---

1. The lobes of foie gras that we buy come in *sous-vide* bags. The foie gras will be hard from being in the fridge, so leave it out overnight at room temperature, still in its bag, to soften it a little.

2. The next day take it from its bag and split the lobe open. Upturn a rounded bowl and cover with a damp cloth. Place each lobe of foie gras over the bottom of the bowl so that it opens and falls on either side of the bowl. With a paring knife, extract all the veins you can see, taking great care not to damage the lobe too much.

3. Place the foie gras lobes in a suitable roasting tray and sprinkle with salt – 25 g (1 oz) per kg (2¹/₄ lb) – pepper, port and Armagnac.

4. Place in the oven preheated to 150°C/300°F/Gas 2 for about 5-10 minutes until the foie gras is soft and at blood temperature. Much of the livers' fat will run out, and the livers themselves will become a little smaller.

5. Carefully remove the livers from the tray using a fish slice, and drain well on a cloth or kitchen paper. Pat dry.

6. Place the pieces of foie gras in layers in the mould – they will find their own level – and chill in the fridge for 24 hours. The terrine will become firm.

7. To serve, remove from the fridge just before serving, and remove from the mould. Remove the cling film, then cut into slices. Place a slice in the middle of each plate, and pipe Madeira jelly around the edges. Serve with toast.

Terrine of Pork Knuckle and Foie Gras, Sauce Gribiche

The terrine of foie gras (previous recipe) which forms layers in this terrine should be started two days in advance.

This terrine also needs to settle for a day.

Use the same size of terrine as in the previous recipe, and line it similarly with cling film.

---

18 portions

4 whole pork knuckles
500 g (18 oz) haricots blancs
a piece of smoked bacon,
  about 75 g (3 oz)
1 carrot
1 celery stalk
1 leek
1 bay leaf
1 sprig fresh thyme
4 litres (7 pints) Chicken
  Stock (basic 2)

½ Terrine of Foie Gras
  (see page 36), halved
  and sliced horizontally

Garnish
2 tablespoons Sauce
  Gribiche per person
  (basic 28)

---

1. Place the pork knuckles, beans and bacon in a large pan. Trim the vegetables and add whole, along with the herbs. Pour in the stock, cover, and cook gently for 2½ hours.

2. Remove the pork, and carefully remove the skins. Keep the skins whole. Flake the meat.

3. Line the cling-filmed terrine mould with the pork knuckle skins.

4. Drain the cooking liquor into a pan, and reduce down by about half to a syrupy glaze. Keep the beans, but pick out and discard the vegetables and herbs.

5. On the base of the lined terrine mould make a layer of the flaked pork, then sprinkle with a little of the reduced liquor. Put in a layer of the beans and a little more liquor, then top with one of the slices of foie gras terrine. Top with another layer of pork and so on, and carry on untii the terrine is full and the ingredients have been used up.

6. Place a piece of greaseproof paper or foil on top of the terrine and weight down. Chill for 24 hours before serving.

7. Remove from the mould, remove the cling film, and cut into slices. Spoon some sauce into the centre of each plate, and arrange a slice of terrine on top.

TIP

Sauce Gribiche is an excellent garnish for this dish and will last a couple of days in the fridge.

Terrine of Vegetables and Langoustines with Caviar

Start this terrine at least 24 hours in advance.

Use the same size of terrine as on page 36, and line it similarly with cling film.

---

18 portions

16 langoustines, no. 2
60 medium leeks, trimmed
salt and freshly ground white
   pepper
30 baby courgettes, trimmed
30 baby carrots, peeled
30 green beans, topped and
   tailed
3 large fennel bulbs, trimmed
   and leaves separated

Garnishes
Water Vinaigrette (basic 31)
green beans split lengthwise
   (optional)
a little caviar (optional)

---

1. Cook the langoustines for 1½-2 minutes in boiling water, then drain and shell. (Keep the shells for making stocks, sauces etc.) Cool.

2. Cook the leeks in salted water until soft, then drain very well and leave to cool.

3. Cook all the remaining vegetables separately in seasoned water until just tender, but keep testing with the point of a sharp knife. Drain very well, and leave to cool.

4. Place a layer of leeks in the bottom of the lined terrine, then top with two lines of the langoustine tails along the length of the terrine. Fill in the gaps lengthways with a layer of courgettes. On top place a layer of leeks. Continue with the langoustine and leeks, with the carrots, beans and fennel, until the ingredients are used up and the terrine is full.

5. Fold over the overlapping lengths of cling film and make two small 2.5 cm (1 in) slits in the top (this helps the terrine to breathe and expel air, preventing bubbles). Place a heavy weight on top, and let rest in a cool place for at least 24 hours.

6. Remove from the mould, and remove the cling film. Cut in slices and place one slice centrally per plate. If you like, decorate with blanched half moons of split beans around the edges. Sprinkle with the vinaigrette and top with a little caviar.

FISH DISHES

Turbot Poché, Mussel and Clam Provençale, Grilled New Potatoes, Sauce Bouillabaisse

Make the stock and sauces well in advance.

---

1 portion

15 g (½ oz) unsalted butter
2 shallots, finely chopped
60 ml (2¼ fl oz) Fish Stock
 (basic 7)
1 tablespoon dry white wine
salt and freshly ground white
 pepper
1 x 175 g (6 oz) fillet of turbot

Garnishes
5 new potatoes
olive oil
50 g (2 oz) each of fresh
 mussels and clams,
 prepared
200 g (7 oz) Tomato Fondue
 (basic 34), fairly dry
4 tablespoons Bouillabaisse
 Sauce (basic 19)
1 tablespoon Rouille 1
 (basic 24)

---

1. Boil the potatoes in salted water until still firm. Drain then slice widthways about 3-5 mm (⅛–¼ in) thick. Drizzle the slices with a little olive oil, then place on a red-hot griddle. Cook for a second, then turn over on to the other side. Turn back again so that the slices have a nice brown, criss-cross pattern on them. Keep warm.

2. Cook the mussels and clams separately in a little water in a covered pan for a minute or so only, until they open. Remove from their shells. (Retain the juices, strain well, and freeze for use in stocks and sauces etc.)

3. Heat the tomato fondue gently in a little olive oil, then add the mussels and clams. Season and keep warm.

4. Bring the bouillabaisse sauce to the boil in a separate pan, then whisk in the rouille. Keep warm.

5. Melt the butter in a small ovenproof pan and sweat the shallots for a minute or two to soften. Add the fish stock, wine and a little salt and pepper.

6. Bring to the boil, place the fish on top, cover with a butter paper and poach in the oven preheated to 220°C/425°F/ Gas 7 for 4-5 minutes only.

7. Arrange the mussels and clams in the middle of the plate, and top with the fish. Spoon the sauce around, and place the chequered ovals of potato in a semi-circle at the top.

Tranche of Turbot Mouginoise, Roast Salsify, Jus Sauternes

Make the mouginoise and sauce in advance.

1 portion

1 x 150 g (5 oz) fillet of turbot
25 g (1 oz) Mouginoise (basic 63)
salt and freshly ground white pepper

Garnishes
50 ml (2 fl oz) Sauternes Sauce (basic 17)
60 g (2¼ oz) unsalted butter
5 or so cloves Confit of Garlic (basic 43)
1 portion Roast Salsify (basic 54)
25 g (1 oz) trompettes de mort

1. Have the garnishes ready before you start to cook the fish.

2. Spread the mouginoise mixture over the turbot fillet, then wrap firmly in cling film.

3. Steam the fish for 6 minutes, 3 minutes on each side.

4. Meanwhile warm the Sauternes sauce through in a small pan. Add 10 g (¼ oz) of the butter, stir in, then season and whisk.

5. Warm the garlic and the salsify.

6. Melt the remaining butter in a small pan, and sweat the trompettes de mort to soften. Drain well.

7. Remove the fish from the cling film, season and place on a hot plate. Surround with the sauce, and garnish with the salsify, garlic cloves and trompettes de mort.

Escalope of Turbot with Girolles, Confit of Garlic

Make the stock and garlic confit well in advance.

1 portion

1 x 175 g (6 oz) fillet of turbot
15 g (1/2 oz) unsalted butter
salt and freshly ground white pepper

Garnishes
1 teaspoon finely chopped shallot

1/2 garlic clove, crushed
a little olive oil
75 g (3 oz) small girolles
60 ml (21/4 fl oz) Double Chicken Stock (basic 2)
30 g (11/4 oz) unsalted butter
1 teaspoon double cream
6 cloves Confit of Garlic (basic 43)

1. For the sauce, sweat off the shallot and garlic in the oil for a few minutes.
2. Add the girolles and cook until the moisture has evaporated from them, but without colouring.
3. Add the chicken stock and boil to reduce by half.
4. Add the butter and then the cream, and season to taste.
5. Heat the garlic cloves through.
6. In a hot frying pan cook the turbot in the butter on both sides, for 6 minutes altogether. Season and keep warm.
7. To serve, put the turbot on a hot plate. Pour the girolle sauce around it, and dot the plate with the hot garlic cloves.

Feuillantine de Saint-Jacques, Copeaux de Fenouil et Infusion de Citronelle

Jean-Christophe Novelli, Four Seasons Hotel, London

Jean-Christophe has been a great friend of mine since we were boys new to the world of cooking. He has supported me in everything I've gone through in the last few years.

4 portions

24 medium scallops, prepared (keep the corals and any trimmings, apart from the black sac, for the sauce)
6 sheets filo pastry
4 egg yolks, beaten
salt and freshly ground white pepper
2 lemongrass stalks, trimmed and finely sliced (keep the trimmings)
juice of 1/2 lemon or 1 lime
16 baby fennel bulbs, trimmed, or 2 medium bulbs, each trimmed and cut into 8 pieces
16 small asparagus stalks, trimmed
50 g (2 oz) unsalted butter

4 medium tomatoes, skinned, seeded and diced
olive oil
a few chervil leaves

Sauce
50 g (2 oz) button mushrooms, sliced
50 g (2 oz) shallots, sliced
50 g (2 oz) celery stalks, sliced
50 g (2 oz) fennel bulb, sliced
50 g (2 oz) unsalted butter
250 ml (8 fl oz) Noilly Prat
120 ml (4 fl oz) dry white wine
250 ml (8 fl oz) Fish Stock (basic 7)
120 ml (4 fl oz) double cream
juice of 1/2 lemon

1. *Pastry* Place one sheet of filo pastry on a lightly floured table. Lightly egg wash it, and place another filo sheet on top. Egg wash again, top with a third filo sheet, and egg wash. Leave to dry. Repeat with the remaining three sheets of filo.
2. When the filo is dry, cut out twelve circles, six from each egg-washed layered filo sheet. Place these on a baking tray, top with another tray, and bake in the oven preheated

to 150°C/300°F/Gas 2, until golden brown, about 10-15 minutes. Leave to cool.

3. *Sauce* Sweat the sliced mushroom, shallot, celery and fennel in a little of the butter for a few minutes. Add the Noilly Prat and wine and boil to reduce by about two-thirds.

4. Sauté the scallop and lemon grass trimmings in a little more of the butter until brown. Add with the fish stock, and boil to reduce again, by about half.

5. Add the cream and reduce to a good sauce consistency. Slowly melt in the remaining butter, cut into dice, then season and add the lemon juice. Pass through a fine sieve and keep warm.

6. *Scallops* Season the scallops, then pan-fry in a hot pan for a few seconds. Add the sliced lemongrass, some of the lemon or lime juice, and a little of the sauce. Turn off the heat.

7. Cook the fennel in boiling salted water for about 3 minutes, and cook the asparagus for 1, then drain both of them. Toss in about half the butter, then season with salt and pepper to taste.

8. Toss the tomato dice in the remaining hot butter, then season.

9. *To serve* Place one of the filo circles in the middle of a plate. Place three scallops on top with two pieces each of fennel and asparagus, and some lemongrass. Coat with a little of the hot sauce.

10. Place another filo circle on top and repeat as above with scallops, fennel, asparagus, lemongrass and sauce. Sprinkle some of the tomato dice around the outside edges.

11. Lightly brush the third filo circle with olive oil then place on top. Garnish with a little chervil.

Panaché of John Dory and Grilled Sea Scallop, Etuvée of Leeks, Sauce Lie de Vin

Make the sauce and the vegetable garnishes in advance.

1 portion

2 x 75 g (3 oz) fillets of John Dory
1 large sea scallop, out of its shell
salt and freshly ground white pepper
1 tablespoon olive oil

Garnishes
1 tablespoon Creamed Parsley (basic 36)
1/2 portion Etuvée of Leeks (basic 52)
50 ml (2 fl oz) Sauce Lie de Vin (basic 18)
1 tablespoon double cream
15 g (1/2 oz) unsalted butter

1. Warm through the creamed parsley and the leeks.
2. Season and fry the John Dory fillets on both sides in the oil in a hot pan, about 3-4 minutes. Make sure the fillets are golden brown on both sides.
3. Griddle or grill the scallop for about the same time.
4. Bring the sauce to the boil in a small saucepan. Add the cream, whisk in the butter, and season to taste.
5. To serve, place the leeks at one side of the warm plate, the parsley at the other. Place the fish on the leeks, the scallop on the parsley. Pour the sauce around.

Grilled Lobster with Garlic Butter, Sauce Choron

Make the court bouillon and garlic butter well in advance; the sauce no more than an hour in advance. Chill the butter.

1 portion

1 x 600 g (1¼ lb) Scottish lobster	Garnishes
Court Bouillon to cover (basic 10)	200 g (7 oz) Garlic Butter (basic 61), chilled
salt and freshly ground white pepper	100 ml (3½ fl oz) Sauce Choron (basic 21)
	sprigs of fresh chervil

1. Bring the court bouillon to the boil in a suitable pan, and cook the lobster for 4 minutes.

2. Remove the lobster from the liquid and take off the claws. Crack these open carefully and remove all the meat.

3. Cut the body of the lobster straight down the middle and remove the brain. Take the tail flesh out of both halves.

4. Slice the tail flesh into medallions and return to the *opposite* side of the shell, so that the red of the meat shows. Put the claw meat into the brain cavities.

5. Put the hard garlic butter in slices on the fish and place under the preheated grill. Grill until the lobster is cooked and the butter melted – about 2-3 minutes – then remove to the serving plate.

6. Heat the sauce gently, then pour over the lobster. Garnish with chervil.

Fillet of Red Mullet with Ratatouille, Sauce Tapenade

Make the ratatouille the day before.

The tapenade lasts well in the fridge. The sauce can be made in the morning.

Cook the fish and fry the beignets at the last minute.

---

1 portion

2 red mullet fillets, approx. 150 g (5 oz) each	Garnishes
salt and freshly ground white pepper	**65 ml (2½ fl oz) Tapenade Sauce (basic 16)**
25 ml (1 fl oz) olive oil	**2 tablespoons Ratatouille (basic 55)**
	2 Beignets of Sage (basic 56)

---

1. Carefully remove the pin bones from the mullet fillets.

2. Bring the sauce to a simmer, and check the seasoning.

3. Warm through the ratatouille.

4. Season the mullet fillets, and pan-fry them in the olive oil for approximately 2½ minutes on the flesh side without colouring, then 1½ minutes on the skin side.

5. Meanwhile, deep-fry the beignets of sage. Drain well.

6. Place the fish on a warm plate. Pass the tapenade sauce through a fine sieve around the fish, and garnish with the ratatouille, shaped in a 5-7 cm (2-3 in) ring mould. Top each fillet with a deep-fried beignet of sage.

TIP

Pan-fried red mullet fillets can also be served with Sauce Vierge (basic 26), or Sauce Antiboise (basic 27). Pomme Fondant, Pomme Boulangère or Confit of Fennel (Garnishes 44, 46, 53) could replace the ratatouille.

Red Mullet with Langoustines, Salad of Herbs and Truffle Vinaigrette

1 portion

2 red mullet fillets, approx. 150 g (5 oz) each	Garnish
salt and freshly ground white pepper	**50 g (2 oz) mixed herb leaves (chervil, tarragon, chives, basil, coriander)**
5 langoustines, no. 1, blanched in boiling water for 1 minute	**1 tablespoon Truffle Vinaigrette (basic 32)**
2 medium leeks, trimmed	
olive oil	

1. Season the mullet fillets, and remove the langoustine tails from their shells.

2. Separate the white and green of the leeks. Wrap the langoustine tails in the white of the leek. Cut the green of the leeks into thin strips (*julienne*).

3. Separately, in olive oil, fry the wrapped langoustines until they start to colour, and the *julienne* of green leeks until they soften, about 1-2 minutes.

4. Fry the mullet fillets in a little olive oil on both sides for 3-4 minutes altogether. Drain.

5. Wash, drain and dry the herb salad.

6. To serve, arrange the mullet fillets and langoustine tails on a plate.

7. Decorate attractively with a 'bouquet' of herb salad, and sprinkle the plate with the vinaigrette and the *julienne* of leeks.

Sea Bass and Blini

Eugene and Tom McCoy, McCoy's, Staddlebridge, N. Yorks.

Tom and Eugene are two of my greatest friends and their restaurant is my favourite place in the whole of Britain, almost a second home to me.

---

1 portion

1 x 175 g (6 oz) fillet of sea bass
1 x 2.5 cm (1 in) thick slice from a medium aubergine
salt
1 tablespoon soured cream
1 teaspoon finely chopped raw onion (optional)

1 dessertspoon best caviar
1 teaspoon chopped fresh parsley
a pinch of grated lemon zest

Garnish (optional)
a little lightly cooked spinach

---

1. Remove the skin from the sea bass fillet and grill this gently until crisp. Set aside.

2. Salt the aubergine lightly and bake in the oven preheated to 180°C/350°F/Gas 4 until golden brown; or grill on both sides.

3. Steam the fish until just cooked, or just firm to the touch, about 3 minutes.

4. Mix the soured cream with the chopped raw onion, if used, and spoon on to the aubergine 'blini'. Top with the caviar.

5. Arrange the steamed fish on a warm plate on top of the spinach (if using). Sprinkle with the crumbled crisp fish skin, the parsley and lemon zest. Place the blini alongside, and serve immediately.

Roast Sea Bass with Tapenade, Confit of Fennel and Herbs, Sauce Vierge

Make the tapenade well in advance.

Make the confit of fennel a few hours beforehand.

---

1 portion

1 x 175 g (6 oz) fillet of sea bass	Garnishes
1 tablespoon olive oil	1 teaspoon Tapenade (basic 37)
salt and freshly ground white pepper	2 tablespoons Sauce Vierge (basic 26)
	a few sprigs of fresh mixed herbs (chervil, chives)
	1 portion Confit of Fennel (basic 53)

---

1. Have the garnishes ready and warming through (if appropriate) before you start cooking the fish.

2. Heat the oil in a pan, and seal the seasoned sea bass on both sides, then cook for 3 minutes on each side.

3. Remove the fillet from the pan and wipe off excess oil.

4. Spread the fillet with the tapenade on the skin side, then place in the centre of a hot plate.

5. Spoon the sauce around the fish, and scatter the plate with the fresh herbs. Garnish with the pieces of fennel and olives.

TIP

Roast sea bass could also be served with Pomme Boulangère (basic 46) – sit the fillet on top of the ring of potatoes – and you could deep-fry some basil leaves as a final garnish.

Confit of Salmon with Tian of Aubergine, Beurre de Tomate

Make the tian of aubergine in the morning and heat up at the last minute.

The 'tomato butter' is best if freshly made.

---

1 portion

1 x 250 g (9 oz) escalope of fresh salmon	Garnishes
goose fat to cover	1 Tian of Aubergine (basic 49)
salt and freshly ground white pepper	50 ml (2 fl oz) puréed cherry tomatoes
sea salt flakes (*fleur de sel*)	1 teaspoon olive oil
	1 teaspoon tomato ketchup
	30 g (1¼ oz) unsalted butter

---

1. Make sure that the salmon escalope is completely boneless.

2. Warm the goose fat on top of the stove in a pan large enough to compactly hold the fish. When at a medium heat, submerge the salmon. Poach for about 4 minutes.

3. Warm the tian of aubergine through.

4. Warm the tomato pulp through gently in a small saucepan. Add the olive oil and ketchup, then whisk in the butter. Season and keep warm.

5. Remove the salmon from the fat and drain well on a clean cloth or kitchen paper.

6. Place the salmon on a hot plate and surround with the tomato sauce. Sprinkle the fish with a few flakes of sea salt, and garnish with the tian of aubergine.

TIP

Confit of Salmon could alternatively be accompanied by Ratatouille (basic 55) or Tapenade Sauce (basic 16).

Escalope de Saumon à l'Estragon

Make the stock, sauce and vegetable garnish in advance.

1 portion

1 x 150 g (5 oz) escalope of salmon
salt and freshly ground white pepper
1 tablespoon olive oil

Garnishes
50 ml (2 fl oz) Velouté for Fish (basic 14)
100 ml (3½ fl oz) Jus de Nage (basic 9)
20 small tarragon leaves, finely snipped
15 g (½ oz) unsalted butter

1. Bring the velouté sauce and nage to the boil together in a saucepan and add the tarragon. Leave to infuse for 10 seconds.

2. Stir in and melt the butter, then season the sauce to taste.

3. Meanwhile, season the salmon and fry in the oil in a non-stick pan for 2 minutes on each side.

4. To serve, pour the sauce into the centre of a warm plate and place the salmon on top.

TIP

Escalope of Salmon would also be good with a velouté flavoured with basil julienne. Etuvée of Fennel and Endive (basic 52) would be a good accompaniment.

Tranche of Cod Viennoise, Sabayon of Grain Mustard

Make the stock, fondue, duxelles and soft herb crust in advance.

Make the velouté for the sabayon in advance; transform it into a sabayon at the last minute.

---

1 portion

1 x 150 g (5 oz) piece of cod fillet

salt and freshly ground white pepper

1 teaspoon Dijon mustard

1 teaspoon Tomato Fondue (basic 34)

1 teaspoon Mushroom Duxelles (basic 64)

50 g (2 oz) Soft Herb Crust (basic 62)

100 ml (3½ fl oz) white wine

100 ml (3½ fl oz) Fish Stock (basic 7)

olive oil

lemon juice

Garnish

1 portion Sabayon of Grain Mustard (basic 15)

---

1. Season the piece of cod, then lightly spread the top with Dijon mustard then the tomato fondue, then the mushroom duxelles.

2. Top all this with the soft herb crust, then place on a butter paper in a shallow ovenproof dish.

3. Add the white wine, fish stock and a splash of olive oil to the pan. Season this cooking liquid with salt and pepper and a little lemon juice.

4. Bring to the boil on top of the stove, then place in the oven preheated to 220°C/425°F/Gas 7 and cook for about 5 minutes.

5. Meanwhile, make the sabayon.

6. To serve, place the cod on a warm plate and pour the sauce around. Place under a preheated grill until the crust and sauce are a golden brown colour. This should take approximately 1 minute.

Smoked Haddock with Poached Egg and New Potatoes

Everything must be prepared and cooked just before serving.

---

1 portion

**1 x 200 g (7 oz) piece of
   naturally smoked haddock
warm milk to cover
salt and freshly ground white
   pepper**

Garnishes
**Mustard Beurre Blanc (basic
   22)
5 medium new potatoes
1 teaspoon white wine
   vinegar
1 egg
sprigs of chervil**

---

1. Make the mustard beurre blanc and keep warm.

2. Cook the new potatoes in boiling salted water until tender. Slice and season. Keep warm.

3. Place the fish in a shallow pan and cover with warm milk. Cook for about 5 minutes, or until the skin peels off easily, then remove from the milk and take off the skin. Keep warm.

4. Bring a small pan of water to the boil, add the vinegar, and poach the egg.

5. To serve, make a bed of sliced potatoes for the fish, then place the egg on top of the fish. Garnish with chervil.

MEAT DISHES

Daube de Boeuf Bourguignonne

The daube can be made a day in advance.

4-6 portions

2.75 kg (6 lb) ox cheek
1 medium onion
1 large carrot
3 celery stalks
1 large leek
1 head of garlic
1 sprig fresh thyme
1 bay leaf
1½ bottles Georges Duboeuf Beaujolais

salt and freshly ground white pepper
about 50 ml (2 fl oz) olive oil
Veal Stock to cover (basic 3)

Garnishes
Garniture Bourgogne (basic 58)
Parsnip Purée (basic 51)

1. Trim the ox cheek of all fat and cut each cheek into three or four pieces. Place in a large dish.

2. Peel and trim the vegetables as appropriate, then cut into large dice. Add to the meat along with the peeled garlic and the herbs, and cover with the red wine. Cover with cling film and leave to marinate in a cool place for 8-12 hours.

3. Drain the meat, keeping the wine and the vegetables. Pass the wine through a sieve and boil to reduce it by half.

4. Dry the meat and vegetables well. Season the meat and colour all over in half the oil in a very hot pan. Drain and place in a suitable casserole. Colour and caramelise the vegetables in the remaining oil, then drain well and add to the meat.

5. Add the reduced red wine to the casserole, then pour in enough veal stock to cover the meat and vegetables. Bring to the boil, then cook in the oven preheated to 180°C/350°F/Gas 4 for 4 hours.

6. Remove from the oven and allow the meat to cool in the liquor. When cold, remove any fat. Reheat gently at the same temperature to serve.

7. Heat the garniture elements separately, and sprinkle over each portion. Serve with a mound of parsnip purée.

Braised Oxtail in Crépinette, Fumet of Red Wine

Start this a day or so ahead.

---

4 portions

2.25 kg (5 lb) oxtail, jointed
750 ml (1¼ pints) red wine
vegetable oil
salt and freshly ground white pepper
3 large carrots, washed
2 large onions
3 celery stalks, washed
1 whole head of garlic
50 ml (2 fl oz) cooking brandy
30 g (1¼ oz) plain flour
2.5 litres (4¼ pints) Veal Stock (basic 3)
a sprig of fresh thyme

1 bay leaf
1 small celeriac
200 g (7 oz) caul fat (*crépinette*)

Sauce
500 ml (17 fl oz) red wine
150 ml (5 fl oz) port
25 g (1 oz) unsalted butter
1 teaspoon double cream

Garnishes
Pomme Purée (basic 45)
Parsnip or Celeriac Purée (basic 51)
Vichy Carrots (basic 50)

---

1. Trim any excess fat from the outside of the pieces of oxtail, then marinate in the red wine overnight.

2. Drain well, and pat the oxtail dry on a cloth. Pass the red wine through a fine sieve, place in a pan on the stove and boil to reduce by three-quarters.

3. Coat the base of a large, thick-bottomed pan with vegetable oil, and heat until almost smoking. Season the oxtail pieces with salt and pepper and seal them all over in the hot oil until they are a good deep, dark colour. Drain.

4. Peel two of the carrots, and both the onions, and cut them and the celery into large pieces. Cut the garlic head in half.

5. Gently roast the chopped vegetables and garlic in the same oil in the pan until they are golden brown.

6. Add the brandy to this and cook until it has almost disappeared.

7. Add the reduced red wine marinade, skimmed of any impurities, and continue to reduce.

8. When almost reduced to a syrup, add the sealed oxtail pieces and stir into the syrupy wine.

9. Sprinkle in the flour (browned in a dry pan for extra flavour if you like), and stir together. Continue to cook for 5 minutes.

10. Pour in 2 litres (3½ pints) of the veal stock, bring to the boil and turn down to a gentle simmer. Add the thyme and bay leaf, cover with a lid and cook gently either on top of the stove or in the oven preheated to 160°C/325°F/Gas 3, for approximately 5 hours or until tender and the meat comes easily off the oxtail bones.

11. Drain the oxtail from the cooking liquid and remove and discard all the pieces of vegetable.

12. Pass the cooking liquid through a fine strainer and then through muslin cloth about three or four times to remove all the impurities and solids.

13. Take one-third of the cooking liquid and reduce it on the stove until very thick. Remove and keep warm. The other two-thirds will be used to make the sauce (see below).

14. Remove all the meat carefully from the oxtails, keeping it in fairly large pieces rather than flakes. Leave behind as much fat and gristle as possible.

15. Peel the celeriac and the remaining carrot and cut them into 1.5 cm (3/4 in) dice. Cook these separately in a little of the hot vegetable oil until golden brownish. Drain and cool.

16. Add the above vegetable dice and the reduced third of the cooking liquid to the pieces of oxtail. Gently combine and allow to cool.

17. When cool, mould the mixture into four portion-size balls. A 120 ml (4 fl oz) ladle is good for this. Then wrap the balls individually in cling film and allow to 'set' in the fridge.

18. When using caul fat, make sure it is well washed and that all the blood is removed. The best way to do this is to sit it under cold running water for about 8 hours.

19. Cut the caul fat into four pieces without holes or large veins of fat. Lay one piece flat on the work surface. Unwrap one oxtail 'ball' from its cling film and place on the caul fat. Roll the caul fat around the ball and tie the two ends of the caul fat together under the ball. Do the same with the remaining balls.

20. To make the sauce, reduce the red wine and port together until a syrup, and then add the remaining two-thirds of the cooking liquor. Reduce this until of a consistency that will coat the back of a spoon.

21. Whisk the hard butter into the sauce to enrich it and give it a glossy shine, then add the cream. This helps stabilise the sauce. Keep to one side.

22. To reheat the oxtail balls, place them in the remaining veal stock in a small saucepan – the stock should cover them by one-third – and put in the oven preheated to 220°C/425°F/Gas 7 for a minimum of 10 minutes. Coat them continually with the stock so that they have a glaze.

23. Reheat the sauce and correct the seasoning. Heat the garnish vegetables.

24. Serve an oxtail ball on a puddle of the sauce – with a little on top as well – with the garnish pomme purée, parsnip or celeriac purée, Vichy carrots or other vegetable of your choice.

Blanquette de Veau à l'Ancienne

The blanquette could be prepared the day before.

4-6 portions

3.75 kg (8 lb) flank of veal
1 medium onion, diced
1 carrot, diced
1 leek, diced
1 whole head of garlic, cloves diced
olive oil
2.25 litres (4 pints) Chicken Stock (basic 1)
375 ml (13 fl oz) double cream
75-100 g (3-4 oz) unsalted butter, chilled

salt and freshly ground white pepper

Garnishes
20-30 new potatoes (5 per person)
225 g (8 oz) mange tout
225 g (8 oz) large spring onions
100 g (4 oz) unsalted butter
225 g (8 oz) girolles
1 medium truffle, cut into thin batons

---

1. Remove any bones from the veal, and trim off the skin and excess fat, but leave a thin layer of fat all over. Cut the meat into 4-5 cm (1½-2 in) cubes. Place in a pan, cover with cold water, and bring to the boil. Skim well, then drain and rinse in cold water. Dry.

2. Sweat the onion, carrot, leek and garlic cloves gently in the olive oil in a suitable casserole. Do not colour.

3. Place the meat on top of the vegetables and cover with the chicken stock. Bring to the boil, cover with a piece of greaseproof paper then the lid, and braise in the oven pre-heated to 160°C/325°F/Gas 3 for 3-3½ hours.

4. Prepare the garnish vegetables. Cook the potatoes in boiling salted water until tender. Top and tail the mange tout, and blanch them in boiling salted water. Trim the onions, leaving about 1-1.5 cm (½-¾ in) of the green stalk on. Cook them in a small pan in an emulsion of half the butter and enough water to cover: cook until glazed and the liquid has disappeared. Trim the girolles, and sauté them in the remaining butter. Keep them all warm.

5. When the meat is cooked, remove it to a plate using a slotted spoon. Pick off and discard the vegetables and herbs. Keep warm.

6. Take half of the cooking liquor – you should have just over a litre (2 pints) – and boil to reduce it by one-third. Add the cream (basically, you are *replacing* that lost third of stock), and continue to reduce until the sauce coats the back of a spoon.

7. Cut the chilled butter into cubes and add them to the sauce. Allow them to melt in gently.

8. Arrange five or so pieces of the veal on the bottom of a large soup bowl, then pour over some of the sauce. Scatter liberally with the mange tout, small onions and girolles. Sprinkle with the batons of truffle, and serve the potatoes separately on a small side plate.

Braised Beef Brisket in a Barley Broth

Mark Prescott, Le Gavroche, London

Another northerner, like me, Mark has worked very hard in this life, and is a great cook. He has perhaps never had the recognition he deserves but maybe he doesn't want it. He is the backbone of the Gavroche, a good man to sit with and talk about food.

---

4 portions

1 x 1.35 kg (3 lb) piece salted
   lean beef brisket, rolled
Chicken Stock to cover
   (basic 1)
salt and freshly ground white
   pepper
400 g (14 oz) best-quality
   pearl barley
1 head green celery
6 medium carrots
2 large leeks

2 turnips
25 g (1 oz) salted butter
2 tablespoons each of
   chopped fresh parsley
   and chives

Garnishes
Pomme Purée (basic 45)
1 bunch spring onions, finely
   chopped

---

1. Place the beef in a suitable casserole, cover with chicken stock, and season. Bring to the boil, cover, and simmer gently for 1½ hours.

2. Add the barley and cook gently for another hour.

3. Wash and peel the vegetables and slice into even, neat, thin squares (*paysanne*). When the barley is nearly cooked, add the vegetables to the broth, and cook for a few minutes only.

4. Check the seasoning of the broth, then add the butter and the chopped herbs just before serving.

5. Serve slices of the meat with some of the vegetables and sauce, along with the hot potato purée mixed with the spring onions.

Pot Roast of Pig's Head with Honey and Cloves

This dish can be made the day before.

---

6 portions

1 pig's head
2 large onions
2-3 large carrots
2 tablespoons olive oil
250 g (9 oz) liquid honey
salt and freshly ground
    white pepper
1 litre (1³/4 pints) each of Veal
    Stock and Chicken Stock
    (basics 3, 1)
20 cloves
2 sprigs fresh thyme

1 bay leaf
a dash of white wine vinegar
1 shallot, finely chopped
15 g (¹/2 oz) clarified butter
15 g (¹/2 oz) unsalted butter

Garnishes
75 g (3 oz) asparagus spears
75 g (3 oz) baby leeks
75 g (3 oz) baby carrots
fresh chervil

---

1. Get your butcher to cut the pig's head in two and remove the brain and tongue whole. Reserve the brain. Put the head and tongue in a large pan of cold water and bring to the boil. Drain and refresh in cold water. Remove to a suitable casserole.

2. Brown the unpeeled onions and the whole carrots in the oil in a separate large saucepan. Add the honey and stir over heat to caramelise the vegetables.

3. Add to the pig's head and tongue in the casserole, and turn over heat to glaze. Season.

4. Cover with the stocks, add 16 of the cloves, 1 sprig of thyme and the bay leaf, and place in the oven preheated to 150°C/300°F/Gas 2. Pot-roast for about 3¹/2 hours, or until the jaw bone starts to loosen from the joint.

5. Meanwhile, cook the brain. Remove the membrane, and cover the brain with water. Add the dash of vinegar, the shallot and the remaining thyme, and bring to the boil. Remove from the heat and let cool in the water. When ready to serve, drain well and pan-fry to a golden brown all over in clarified butter.

6. When the pig's head is cooked, remove the head from the pot and remove the meat from the cheeks, temples and snout. Keep separate with the tongue.

7. Pass the remainder of the cooking juices through a muslin-lined sieve and reduce to a coating sauce. Add the 4 remaining cloves and leave aside to infuse.

8. When ready to serve, heat up the sauce, remove the cloves, and stir in the butter.

9. Lightly cook the garnish vegetables in boiling salted water.

10. Place a little of each of the different pieces of pig's head, including the tongue and brain, on plates. Cover with the sauce and surround with the vegetables. Garnish with the chervil.

Roast Calf's Sweetbread with Broad Beans and Fresh Morels, Velouté Sauce

Make the chicken stock for the sauce well in advance, and the sauce earlier in the day.

Prepare the vegetables in the morning.

---

4 portions

4 x 185 g (6½ oz) calf's sweetbreads	Garnishes
	350 g (12 oz) shelled broad beans
salt and freshly ground white pepper	
	40 fresh morels
100 g (4 oz) unsalted butter	100 g (4 oz) unsalted butter
8 very thin slices Parma ham	Velouté for Fish (basic 14)

---

1. Blanch the broad beans in boiling water for 3 minutes. Remove and discard the greyish skin surrounding the bright green inner bean.

2. Wash the morels very thoroughly in cold salted water, then drain thoroughly. Cut in half if large.

3. Blanch the sweetbreads in boiling salted water for a minute. Trim the membrane and any fatty bits from the sweetbreads.

4. Seal the sweetbreads in the hot butter to colour but not cook. Wrap them carefully in the Parma ham, 2 slices per sweetbread, then fry in the same pan and the same fat to crisp the ham. Finish in the oven preheated to 190°C/375°F/Gas 5 for about 6 minutes.

5. Sauté the morels in the butter on a medium heat for 6 minutes, or until tender.

6. Warm the sauce through, and add the broad beans.

7. Place each sweetbread in the middle of a large warm plate, pour the sauce around, and sprinkle with the freshly cooked morels.

Tranche of Calf's Liver, Sauce Bercy

Begin the sauce at least the day before.

4 portions

4 x 175 g (6 oz) thin slices calf's liver	Sauce Bercy (basic 11)
salt and freshly ground white pepper	900 g (2 lb) baby spinach leaves, washed thoroughly
plain flour	50 ml (2 fl oz) water
vegetable oil	50 g (2 oz) unsalted butter
	8 wafer-thin slices streaky bacon
Garnishes	
Pomme Purée (basic 45)	4 large fresh sage leaves

1. Prepare the garnish potato purée and sauce in advance and keep warm.

2. Cook the spinach in the water and butter for a few minutes only until just wilted. Season with salt and pepper, then drain. Keep warm.

3. Grill the bacon until crisp. Deep-fry the sage leaves in hot vegetable oil for a few seconds until crisp. Drain well.

4. Season the raw liver slices with salt and pepper, and flour lightly.

5. Heat 50 ml (2 fl oz) of the vegetable oil in a large wide pan, and fry the liver until golden brown on each side and pink in the middle, about 3-4 minutes in total.

6. Place the spinach in the middle of the warm plate, and arrange the liver on top. Place the crisp bacon on top of the liver along with the sage leaves. Arrange a quenelle of potato at one side of the spinach and liver.

Fillet of Lamb with Herbs, Roasted Shallots and Tarragon Juice

Make the stock and garnishes in advance.

---

4 portions

4 fillets of lamb
salt and freshly ground white pepper
olive oil
200 g (7 oz) fresh white breadcrumbs
200 g (7 oz) fresh parsley, chopped
20 g (³/₄ oz) fresh thyme leaves
4 garlic cloves, chopped
about 40 g (1¹/₂ oz) unsalted butter

4 medium leeks, trimmed
800 ml (1¹/₃ pints) Lamb Stock (basic 4)
a few tarragon leaves
8 tomatoes, skinned, seeded and diced
Garnishes
12 Roast Shallots (basic 42)
4 Pomme Fondant (basic 44)
4 Tians of Aubergine (basic 49)
fresh chervil

---

1. Season the lamb fillets with salt and pepper and seal off on all sides in a little of the olive oil. Allow to cool.

2. Mix the breadcrumbs, parsley, thyme and garlic together, then bind with the butter to make a paste. Coat the fillet with this.

3. Separate the leek leaves, and wrap them around the fillet; tie in place if necessary.

4. Place the lamb stock in a pan and bring to the boil. Reduce the temperature, and poach the leek-wrapped fillets in this for 10 minutes.

5. Meanwhile, prepare and cook or reheat the garnishes – the roast shallots, the fondant potato and the tians of aubergine.

6. Remove the lamb from the stock and keep warm. Boil to reduce the stock by a quarter, then add the tarragon and tomato dice. Season to taste.

7. To serve, slice each fillet in three and arrange attractively on plates.

8. Add the vegetables and pour on the sauce. Garnish with sprigs of fresh chervil.

Rump of Lamb, Provençale Vegetables, Jus Niçois

Make the sauce in advance.

Many of the vegetable garnishes could be prepared in advance.

Some of these don't need recipes – the idea is to have a colourful, flavourful and generous garnish for the lamb.

---

1 portion

1 chump of lamb, about
    225-275 g (8-10 oz) in
    weight
salt and freshly ground white
    pepper
1 tablespoon clarified butter

Garnishes
various simple vegetables
    such as roast potatoes
    (use goose fat for the best
    flavour), roast red and

yellow peppers, and
    grilled slices of
    courgette
2-3 cloves Confit of Garlic
    (basic 43)
1 Tian of Aubergine (basic
    49)
400 ml (14 fl oz) Lamb Sauce
    (basic 4)
10 black olives, stoned and
    finely diced
a knob of unsalted butter

---

1. Take the chump off the bone, skin it and then you are left with a small roasting joint. Season it well.

2. Brown all over in the clarified butter on top of the stove, then roast in the oven preheated to 230°C/450°F/Gas 8 for 8-10 minutes, turning halfway through the cooking time. Rest for about 10-15 minutes.

3. Warm through the vegetable garnishes.

4. Bring the lamb sauce to the boil, check the consistency, then add the olives. Cook for 1 minute, then check the seasoning. Whisk the butter in to give a gloss and slightly enrich.

5. To serve, slice the meat into eight or nine pieces, and fan out across one side of the hot plate. Cover with the sauce, and garnish with the vegetables.

Roast Herbed Chicken with Girolles

Make the sauce in advance.

2 portions

1 good free-range chicken, about 1.5 kg (3¼ lb) in weight	15 g (½ oz) unsalted butter, softened
1 large sprig fresh thyme	Garnishes
1 bunch fresh flat-leaf parsley	Jus of Herbs (basic 12)
4 slices white bread, dried	2 Pomme Fondant (basic 44)
½ garlic clove, crushed	100 g (4 oz) fresh girolles
30 g (1¼ oz) clarified butter	100 g (4 oz) green beans
salt and freshly ground white pepper	about 50 g (2 oz) unsalted butter

1. To prepare the chicken, take out the wishbone and remove the legs and winglets (you can use these in the sauce).

2. Work your hand in between the skin and flesh, following the shape of the chicken from neck to tail, to create a large pouch covering both breasts.

3. To make the herb farce, pick the thyme and parsley leaves off the stalks and blend with the dried bread to make green breadcrumbs. Stir in the crushed garlic, clarified butter and seasoning, and mix to a fine crumb texture.

4. Push the farce gently into the pouch in the bird, so that it is nice and even all round. Place in the fridge so that the farce can set.

5. Have ready the sauce and the potatoes. Keep warm.

6. Moisten the breast with the softened butter and colour to a golden brown on top of the stove. Cover with foil, then roast in the oven preheated to 200°C/400°F/Gas 6 for 12-15 minutes. Rest for about 8 minutes.

7. Meanwhile, wash and trim the girolles and green beans. Cook the girolles for a few minutes in half the butter, and the beans in an emulsion of the remaining butter and some water for 5 minutes. Drain both well. Keep warm.

8. Cut the breasts off the carcass, and place in the middle of each warmed plate. Garnish with the potatoes, girolles and green beans. Pour the sauce carefully around.

Guinea Fowl en Cocotte with Fresh Garden Peas and Morels, Sauce Albufera

Make the stock well in advance, the sauce the day before.

2 portions

1 x 1.5 kg (3¹/₄ lb) guinea fowl	Garnishes
500 ml (17 fl oz) Double Chicken Stock (basic 2)	**Sauce Albufera (basic 13)**
	100 g (4 oz) fresh morels
salt and freshly ground white pepper	**25 g (1 oz) unsalted butter**
25 g (1 oz) unsalted butter, softened	**150 g (5 oz) fresh podded peas**
	6 very thin slices streaky bacon

1. Remove the legs and winglets from the guinea fowl (use these in a sauce).

2. Poach the guinea fowl in the chicken stock for 10 minutes, then remove and allow to rest and cool. Save the stock, using it in the making of the sauce (basic 13), or chill and freeze.

3. Meanwhile, make or warm through the sauce.

4. Wash the fresh morels well and trim them at the base. Sauté in half the butter until nicely cooked, then season with salt. Cook the peas in the remaining butter and a little water to a glaze.

5. Season the breasts of the guinea fowl, then cover evenly with a thin layer of butter. Caramelise evenly in a frying pan, then place in the oven preheated to 200°C/400°F/Gas 6 for 6 minutes to finish the cooking.

6. Grill the slices of bacon until crisp.

7. Take the breasts off the bird and place in the centre of each plate. Arrange the bacon on top and the morels and peas around, and pour the sauce on carefully.

Challans Duck Marco Polo, Green Peppercorns and Caramelised Apples

Make the sauce in advance.

---

2 portions

1 Challans duck, about 1.5 kg (3¹⁄₄ lb) in weight	Garnishes
1 tablespoon olive oil	Sauce Albufera (basic 13)
salt and freshly ground white pepper	2 Pomme Fondant (basic 44)
	12 green peppercorns
	1 Cox's apple
	15 g (¹⁄₂ oz) unsalted butter
	1 large pinch caster sugar

---

1. Remove the legs from the duck (and keep for another dish: they're good roasted and served with a salad as a starter dish).

2. Colour the duck in the oil on top of the stove, then roast in the oven preheated to 200°C/400°F/Gas 6 for 12-15 minutes. Remove from the oven and allow to rest.

3. Warm the sauce and the potatoes. Add the green peppercorns to the sauce just before serving.

4. Peel the apple and cut into six wedges. Turn each wedge a little at the side to make a rounder shape.

5. Melt the butter and sugar together in a small pan, to caramelise, then add the apple wedges. Cook quickly on a fast heat until golden brown.

6. Cut the breasts off the duck and cut into five slices. Place these in the centre of the plate. Garnish with the potatoes and the caramelised apple wedges, then pour the sauce around.

Bresse Pigeon, Braised Cabbage, Mushroom Ravioli and Thyme Juice

Make the stock and confit of garlic well in advance. Make the cabbage and ravioli in the morning.

4 portions

4 Bresse pigeons
about 2 litres (3¹/₂ pints)
   Pigeon Stock (basic 5)
40 g (1¹/₂ oz) fresh thyme
40 ml (1¹/₂ fl oz) each of port,
   Madeira and Armagnac
25 g (1 oz) unsalted butter
salt and freshly ground white
   pepper

Garnishes
Braised Cabbage (basic 48)
8 Mushroom Ravioli (basic
   57)
truffle oil
4 Pomme Fondant (basic 44)
8 cloves Confit of Garlic
   (basic 43)
50 g (2 oz) chanterelles
15 g (¹/₂ oz) unsalted butter
fresh chervil

1. Poach the pigeons gently in the pigeon stock for 18 minutes.

2. Reheat the garnishes while the pigeon is poaching. Braise the cabbage; poach the mushroom ravioli, then toss in truffle oil; heat the potato fondant and garlic through. Sauté the chanterelles in the butter. Keep warm.

3. After the 18 minutes' poaching, drain the pigeons, then remove the breasts, along with the leg and wing bones. Keep the pigeon warm.

4. Add the thyme and alcohols to the pigeon stock and reduce until a sauce consistency. Blend in the butter, and season to taste.

5. To serve, place some warm cabbage on a plate, put the pigeon on top, and cover with sauce.

6. Place the mushrooms in a mound at one side, with the ravioli on top. On the other side of the plate, place the potato and the garlic cloves. Garnish with sprigs of the chervil.

Roast Saddle of Rabbit with Langoustines

The stock can be made well in advance; the langoustines could have been blanched and the vegetables cooked a few hours beforehand.

---

2 portions

1 saddle of rabbit
3 tablespoons clarified butter
salt and freshly ground white
    pepper
8 langoustines, blanched in
    boiling salted water for 1
    minute

Garnishes
200 ml (7 fl oz) Chicken
    Stock (basic 1)
25 g (1 oz) unsalted butter
1 teaspoon whipping cream,
    whipped
1 sprig fresh rosemary
Etuvée of Endive (basic 52)
50 g (2 oz) trompettes de
    mort
1 tablespoon clarified
    butter

---

1. Trim the saddle of rabbit, leaving it on the bone, and cut off the belly flaps. In a suitable ovenproof pan, pan-fry the saddle and belly in 2 tablespoons of the clarified butter until nice and golden.

2. Lift out the saddle, and arrange the belly pieces on the base of the pan. Replace the saddle on top of the belly and roast in the oven preheated to 240°C/475°F/Gas 9 for about 8 minutes. Leave to rest for about 6 minutes.

3. Cut the belly pieces into very thin *julienne* strips and fry in the fat remaining in the pan until very crisp. Drain well and keep warm.

4. Remove the fat from the pan and add the stock. Stir and boil to reduce by half. Whisk in the butter, then the cream, and then leave the rosemary in it for a few minutes, to infuse.

5. Heat through the endive, and pan-fry the trompettes de mort in the clarified butter. Drain the latter and cut into *julienne* strips.

6. Shell the langoustines and roast them in the remaining clarified butter in the hot oven for 1½ minutes.

7. To serve, take the two fillets of rabbit from the bone, cut in half and arrange a piece on either side of each plate, with the crisp belly strips on top. Pour the strained sauce around. Place 4 langoustine tails between each pair of fillets. Sprinkle the endives around, and then the *julienne* of trompettes.

Roast Saddle of Rabbit, Etuvée of Asparagus and Leeks, Jus of Rosemary

Roast the saddle of rabbit as in the previous recipe, and fry the belly *julienne* until crisp. Make the sauce as outlined on the previous page.

Pour the sauce around the saddle pieces, topped with the crisp belly, and arrange asparagus spears and baby leeks (Etuvée of Asparagus and Leeks, basic 52). Garnish with chervil.

TIP

The roast saddle of rabbit can be served with a Herb Risotto (basics 38, 39). Slice the meat and arrange alongside the rice.

Stracci Pasta with Rabbit

Stefano Cavallini, The Halkin, London

Stefano and I have known each other for years, and his is the best Italian restaurant in Britain (but that's only to be expected from someone who has worked with Gualtiero Marchesi, holder of three Michelin stars in Milan). Stefano is probably as crackers as I am.

---

4 portions

2 saddles of rabbit
1 litre (1³/₄ pints) water
50 g (2 oz) carrot, chopped
30 g (1¹/₄ oz) celery, chopped
3 garlic cloves
1 tomato, quartered
1 teaspoon fresh thyme
   leaves
40 g (1¹/₂ oz) unsalted butter
500 ml (17 fl oz) white wine
120 g (4¹/₂ oz) wild
   mushrooms, sliced

Pasta
200 g (7 oz) pasta flour
   (type 00)
4 egg yolks
2 eggs
salt
80 g (3¹/₄ oz) fresh spinach
   leaves, cooked and
   puréed

---

1. Remove the meat from the saddles of rabbit and cut into 2.5 cm (1 in) square pieces. Keep the kidney whole.

2. Cut the rabbit bones into small pieces and roast them in the oven preheated to 240°C/475°F/Gas 9 for 5 minutes. Remove from the oven, put into a saucepan, and add the water, carrots, celery, garlic, tomato and thyme. Simmer for 20 minutes.

3. In the meantime prepare the pasta. Make a well in the middle of half of the flour, and add 3 of the egg yolks, 1 whole egg and a pinch of salt. Mix slowly until the dough comes together, then knead gently for a few minutes.

4. Do exactly the same with the rest of the flour and eggs, but mix in the spinach purée.

5. Firstly roll the white pasta out very thinly, then do the same with the green spinach pasta. Cut both into triangular pieces, the sides roughly 10 cm (4 in).

6. Melt 2 teaspoons of the butter in a saucepan and cook the rabbit dice for a few minutes to brown them. Add the kidney, but cook only until pink. Remove from the pan and keep warm.

7. Remove the butter from the pan, and add the white wine. Bring to the boil, and boil to reduce almost entirely, then add the strained rabbit bone stock. Allow to boil for a further 2-3 minutes then add 20 g ($3/4$ oz) of the remaining butter.

8. In another saucepan, cook the wild mushrooms in the remaining butter, then add to the sauce.

9. Cook the pasta in boiling salted water for a minute or so only. Make sure it is still al dente, and when ready place it in the sauce.

10. Pour this on to individual hot plates, and garnish with the rabbit dice and pieces of the kidney.

Lapin aux Saint-Jacques

Christian Delteuil

In 1981, when I first came to London, I used to spend my wages most Saturdays eating at L'Arlequin. Christian is still a great cook and an inspiration.

---

1 portion

2 x 75 g (3 oz) fillets of rabbit, cut from the saddle
a little olive oil
1 teaspoon ground cumin
salt and freshly ground white pepper
the 2 rabbit kidneys
2 scallops, trimmed and cleaned

50 ml (2 fl oz) red wine vinegar
100 ml (3½ fl oz) Veal Stock (basic 3)
1 tablespoon tiny capers, drained
2 thin slices smoked bacon

Garnish
cauliflower purée

---

1. Marinate the rabbit fillets overnight in a mixture of the olive oil, cumin and seasoning.

2. Place the rabbit kidneys on a small skewer.

3. Slice each of the scallops into four horizontally. Chill to firm.

4. Drain the fillets and roast quickly – for 6 minutes – in the oven preheated to 230°C/450°F/Gas 8. Remove from the oven and keep warm.

5. Deglaze the roasting pan with the vinegar, and reduce to a syrup. Add the veal stock and cook for a few minutes to reduce. Pass through a fine sieve, and add the capers. Keep warm.

6. Briefly grill the kidneys, the scallops and the bacon.

7. Cut the rabbit fillets into fine slices and arrange on the plate, interspersed with the slices of scallop. Pour a little of the sauce around, and top with the grilled slices of bacon. Put the kidneys on their skewer to one side.

PUDDINGS

Champagne Jelly

Make no longer than a day in advance.

4 portions

1 pink grapefruit	Champagne jelly
2 oranges	**½ bottle (325 ml/11½ fl oz)**
1 banana	**Champagne**
1 small punnet raspberries	**300 g (11 oz) caster sugar**
	6 gelatine leaves, soaked in
	cold water to soften

1. To make up the jelly, dissolve the sugar in the Champagne over gentle heat. Remove from the heat and add and melt the gelatine. Strain through a fine sieve and leave to cool.

2. Peel and segment the grapefruit and oranges. Remove excess juice from the segments with an absorbent cloth. Peel and slice the banana into thin discs.

3. Pour a little cooled jelly into the bottom of each of four dariole (or similar) moulds. Place the raspberries point down into the jelly and leave to set.

4. Arrange the banana slices in next, then the orange segments and lastly the grapefruit segments.

5. Fill to the top with jelly, cover with cling film, then leave to set. Turn out to serve (dip the base of the moulds briefly in hot water).

TIP

The jelly can be made with a variety of fruit. Serve with some raspberry coulis (basic 68) or with a sauce made from some orange juice thickened with a little apricot purée (basic 74).

Crème Brûlée

In The Restaurant, we often make crème brûlée in small round, eared dishes (*oeufs sur le plat*). They are not cooked in a bain-marie as here, and need about 50-60 minutes' very gentle cooking at 100°C/212°F/a very low gas. We sometimes use caster sugar instead of demerara, and repeat the sprinkling and grilling for a particularly crunchy topping. The crème brûlées can be made a day in advance.

---

10 portions

150 g (5 oz) caster sugar
10 egg yolks
4 vanilla pods
100 ml (3½ fl oz) milk

900 ml (1½ pints) double cream
demerara sugar

---

1. Mix the sugar and egg yolks together well in a bowl.
2. Split the vanilla pods in half and scrape the seeds out into the milk and cream in a pan. Add the pods too, and heat gently so that the full flavour of the seeds and pods infuses the liquid.
3. Pour the cream and milk on to the yolks, mix well, then pass through a conical strainer.
4. Divide the mixture between ten ramekin dishes (roughly 7.5 cm/3 in in diameter). Cook in a bain-marie of hot water in the oven preheated to 140°C/275°F/Gas 1 for about 30-40 minutes or until just set.
5. Allow to cool and set, then chill in the fridge.
6. Sprinkle the tops with demerara sugar, and glaze under a hot grill (or use a blowtorch). Allow the sugar to set hard, then serve in the dish.

Crème Brûlée, Pommes Sec, Jus de Granny Smith

The crème brûlée here is made in much the same way as that above, but it contains more egg yolks: it must be firmer than the other one because it has to be turned out of its dish.

10 portions

**750 ml (1¼ pints) double
   cream**
250 ml (8 fl oz) milk
140 g (4¾ oz) caster sugar
16 egg yolks

4 vanilla pods, split
brown demerara sugar

Garnish
Granny Smith apples

1. Mix the cream, milk, sugar and egg yolks together in a bowl. Scrape the vanilla seeds into the liquid and add the pods as well. Leave for an hour or so for the vanilla to flavour the liquid, then remove the pods.

2. Pour the mixture into individual small 7.5 cm (3 in) ramekins, place in a bain-marie, and cook in the oven pre-heated to 100°C/212°F/a very low gas, for 1½ hours.

3. Remove from the oven, leave to cool in the bain-marie, then refrigerate. Turn the crème brûlées out of their moulds an hour before serving.

4. Peel, core and very, very thinly slice three of the apples (use a mandoline, so that the slices are virtually transparent). Place on a baking sheet and dry in the oven preheated to 150°C/300°F/Gas 2 for about 45 minutes until they become crisp.

5. Cut three apples per person into four pieces, skin, core and all, and juice in a juicer. Remove the froth.

6. Place the brûlées on a tray or on individual plates. Powder the demerara sugar in a strong processor and sprinkle over the tops of the brûlées. Using a blowtorch, or a preheated grill, caramelise the tops. Clean the plates of any excess sugar.

7. Pierce all round the sides of the brûlées with slices of dried apple, so that each one looks like a fan. Pour the apple 'juice' around the outside of the brûlées.

Crème Vanille and Poached Fruits

You can use a variety of fruits, prepared as appropriate – pears, kiwi, lychees, apricots (basic 75). Poach in the same way as below, using an appropriate liqueur in the syrup. Decorate with the spices used in the poaching.

---

10 portions

1 litre (1¾ pints) double cream
135 g (4¾ oz) caster sugar
7 vanilla pods
3 gelatine leaves, soaked in cold water to soften

Poached strawberries
3 punnets strawberries, hulled
½ bottle Champagne
300 g (11 oz) caster sugar

Poached pineapple
1 medium pineapple, peeled and thinly sliced

Poaching Syrup to cover (basic 67)
Kirsch
2 cinnamon sticks

Poached mango
1 large mango, peeled and thinly sliced
a couple of slices of fresh ginger
Poaching Syrup to cover (basic 67)
Bacardi rum

---

1. Place the cream and sugar in a saucepan. Split the vanilla pods, scrape the seeds into the cream, and add the pods too. Bring to the boil, then put over a bowl of ice.

2. Add the soaked gelatine, which will start to dissolve. Whisk in, then slowly, over a period of time, keep stirring until the mixture starts to set.

3. Pour into moulds – we use dariole moulds, which are about 6.25-7.5 cm (2½-3 in) high, 3.75 cm (1½ in) in diameter at the base. Leave to set completely.

4. For the poached strawberries, bring the Champagne and sugar to the boil together on top of the stove. Pour on to the hulled strawberries in an appropriate dish and leave to cool. Chill.

5. For the poached pineapple, place the pineapple slices in a pan and cover with syrup. Add Kirsch (50ml/2 fl oz per 500 ml/17 fl oz syrup) and the cinnamon. Bring to the boil and simmer for 1 minute. Remove from the heat and leave to cool. Chill.

6. For the poached mango, place the mango and ginger slices in a pan and cover with syrup. Add Bacardi in the same proportions as above. Bring to the boil, then immediately remove from the heat: mango is more delicate than pineapple. Leave to cool, then chill.

7. To unmould, run the dariole sides under hot water for a minute to loosen. Turn the vanilla creams out on to the centre of individual plates. Fan the mango at one side, and the pineapple at the other. Top each with a little of their syrup. Place the strawberries at the top of the plate, adding a little more of their Champagne juices to give colour and incomparable flavour.

TIP

The poached fruits will last for a day or so in the fridge. Make the vanilla cream at the most a day in advance.

Crème Caramel au Raisin Sec

At The Restaurant, we serve tiny versions of this as an *amuse-gueule* before the dessert proper.

Start making the day before.

---

10 portions

1 litre (1¾ pints) milk	Caramel and raisins
200 g (7 oz) caster sugar	**25-40 g (1-1½ oz) raisins**
6 whole eggs	**dark rum to cover**
1 egg yolk	**100 g (4 oz) caster sugar**
vanilla essence	**85 ml (3 fl oz) water**

---

1. Soak the raisins in rum to cover for at least 24 hours.

2. Place the caramel sugar and 25 ml (1 fl oz) of the water in a small pan. Over a high heat, boil to a dark caramel, then add the remaining water. Mix to a viscous caramel.

3. Place a 3-5 mm (⅛-¼ in) layer of caramel in the bottom of each mould – we use dariole moulds. If the moulds are small, add 2-3 marinated raisins; if larger, 7-8 raisins.

4. To make the custard, bring the milk and half the sugar to the boil, then let cool for 5 minutes.

5. Whisk the remaining sugar together with the eggs and the egg yolk. Whisk in the slightly cooled milk.

6. Pass through a fine sieve and add vanilla essence to taste. Fill the moulds to the top.

7. Place the filled moulds in a bain-marie of warm water and cook in the oven preheated to about 130°C/260°F/Gas ½-1 for 45-60 minutes.

8. Allow to cool before unmoulding – run the thin blade of a knife around between the edges of the mould and the custard. Serve as they are.

Nougat Glacé, Sauce of Raspberries

This frozen dessert should be made a day in advance.

It needs a very cold freezer, otherwise the caramel will start to dissolve.

15 portions

425 g (15 oz) caster sugar
150 g (5 oz) shelled hazelnuts
6 egg whites

450 ml (15 fl oz) double
   cream
Raspberry Coulis (basic 68)

1. Line a terrine 30 x 7.5 cm (12 x 3 in) with greaseproof paper. Set the freezer to its coldest.
2. Heat 150 g (5 oz) of the sugar in a heavy-based pan to melt and make a caramel.
3. Stir in the hazelnuts and pour on to a cold oiled tray to set. When cold, crush into small pieces.
4. Whip the egg whites and the remaining sugar together to make a stiff meringue.
5. Whip the cream to stiff peaks, then fold together with the meringue and crushed nuts gently until mixed.
6. Fill the terrine to the top with the mixture, and place in the freezer until hard.
7. To serve, remove the terrine from the freezer. Cut into slices and serve surrounded by the raspberry coulis.

WILD FOOD FROM LAND AND SEA

Soufflé Rothschild

Albert Roux

He was like a father figure to me during my time at Le
Gavroche, and I shall always be grateful to him.

---

1 portion

2 tablespoons Crème	Garnishes
Pâtissière (basic 72)	**4 halves Poached Apricots**
1 tablespoon Cointreau	**(basic 75)**
4 egg whites	**60 ml (2¹/₄ fl oz) Apricot**
100 g (4 oz) caster sugar	**Purée (basic 74)**
about 25 g (1 oz) unsalted	**¹/₂ teaspoon Cointreau**
butter	

---

1. Make and have ready the garnishes in two small pans.
Warm them through gently while the soufflé is being
prepared and cooked. Add the Cointreau to the purée.

2. Put the crème pâtissière and Cointreau in a round-
bottomed bowl and whisk together thoroughly.

3. Put the egg whites in another bowl and whisk to soft peaks.
Add the sugar gradually, whisking in until the mixture is stiff.

4. Take a blini pan, or a small heatproof and ovenproof flat
tin of about 10 cm (4 in) in diameter. Brush it thoroughly with
some of the butter, up and over the sides. Place in the oven
preheated to 180°C/350°F/Gas 4 for 10 minutes to allow it to
become red-hot.

5. Add a quarter of the whipped egg white to the crème
pâtissière and whisk together. Fold in the remaining egg
white carefully.

6. Bring the pan out of the oven and butter again thoroughly. Delicately place the soufflé mixture in the pan and knock
it slightly on the work surface. The pan should be full. Cook
briefly – for 30 seconds – on top of the stove, then place in
the oven for 3¹/₂-4 minutes or until nicely browned.

7. To serve, pour the warm apricot purée on to a plate and
garnish the edges with the poached apricots. Take the soufflé
out of the pan, and turn out, smooth side up, on to the centre
of the plate. Serve immediately.

Prune and Armagnac Soufflé

You could make this soufflé for one, but you would have to whip the egg whites (3 per person) by hand, rather than in a machine.

Divide all the other ingredients by four.

The soufflé could have been frozen; the prunes will have been marinating for at least two weeks.

---

4 portions

50 g (2 oz) unsalted butter
12 egg whites
300 g (12 oz) caster sugar
4 generous dessertspoons
    Prune and Armagnac
    Soufflé Base (basic 77)
4 whole Marinated Prunes
    (basic 76)

Garnishes
4 whole Marinated Prunes
    (basic 76)
Armagnac Crème Anglaise
    (basic 69)

---

1. Grease four 7.5 x 6.25 cm (3 x 2½ in) soufflé dishes well with half the butter. Place in the fridge so that the butter sets hard, then butter again just before pouring in the soufflé mixture.
2. Preheat the oven well to 180°C/350°F/Gas 4.
3. Put the egg whites in the bowl of your mixer or processor, and begin to beat. When they start to take shape, start adding the sugar – a quarter, say, at a time. When mixed in, add another quarter and so on. This is *not* a meringue mix.
4. Put the soufflé base in a rounded bowl, and whisk in a third of the beaten egg white. This loosens the base. Fold in the remaining egg white carefully.
5. Half-fill the soufflé dishes with the mixture, then place a whole marinated prune in the centre. Fill to the top with the mixture, then scrape off evenly with a palette knife. Run your thumb around the edges to push the mixture away from the sides (otherwise it might stick to the sides and not rise).
6. Cook in the preheated oven for 8-10 minutes. The soufflés should be quite firm on the outside, lovely and moist on the inside.
7. Serve in the dish on a plate, with a prune on top, and sauce to the side.

Galette of Peach Filled with Almond Ice Cream on Strawberry Sauce

John Burton-Race, L'Ortolan, Shinfield, Berkshire

I've known John for over ten years now, and he's a great cook – I remember when he won his first star. I used to go and eat his food at Petit Blanc every Monday when I had my day off from Le Manoir.

6 portions

6 ripe peaches (white are best), halved and stoned
6 sprigs fresh mint

Stock syrup
500 ml (17 fl oz) water
120 g (4½ oz) caster sugar

Galettes (shortbread)
90 g (3½ oz) unsalted butter
60 g (2¼ oz) icing sugar
1 egg yolk
120 g (4½ oz) plain flour

Almond ice cream
300 ml (10 fl oz) milk
30 g (1¼ oz) ground almonds
6 egg yolks
100 g (4 oz) caster sugar
300 ml (10 fl oz) double cream

30 g (1¼ oz) white almond paste (or marzipan)
50 ml (2 fl oz) Amaretto (almond liqueur) or good almond essence

Strawberry sauce
2 punnets ripe strawberries, washed and hulled
60 g (2¼ oz) icing sugar

Nougatine
60 g (2¼ oz) caster sugar
50 ml (2 fl oz) glucose syrup
50 g (2 oz) flaked almonds
5 g (⅛ oz) unsalted butter

Spun sugar
100 g (4 oz) caster sugar
2 tablespoons glucose syrup
2 tablespoons water

1. *Syrup* Pour the water into a saucepan and stir in the sugar. Bring to the boil then reduce the heat.
2. Plunge each peach half into the boiling syrup for 15 seconds. Remove from the syrup and put into iced water. Remove the syrup from the heat.
3. The skins from the peaches should easily peel away from the fruit. Place the peeled peaches in the syrup. Chill.

4. *Galettes* Beat the butter and sugar together until pale and creamy. Beat in the egg yolk then beat the flour in to a smooth paste. Put the mixture into a piping bag fitted with a large star nozzle. Pipe six 6 cm (2½ in) rosettes on to a lightly buttered baking tray.

5. Place in the oven preheated to 200°C/400°F/Gas 6, and bake to a golden brown, about 20 minutes. Remove from the oven and leave to cool. When cold remove the galettes with a spatula, and put into an airtight container. Store until required.

6. *Almond ice cream* Bring the milk and ground almonds to the boil. Remove from the heat, cover with a tight fitting lid, and leave to go cold. This is done to infuse the flavour of the ground almonds. Strain the almond milk through a muslin bag, squeezing out every last drop of milk. Discard the almonds and re-measure the milk: you need the full 300 ml (10 fl oz).

7. In a bowl whisk together the egg yolks and sugar until pale in colour.

8. Bring the almond milk and the cream to the boil, then add the almond paste and reduce the heat.

9. Pour a little of the boiled milk and cream over the whisked yolks. Mix together and pour this into the saucepan. Gently cook the sauce until it coats the back of the spoon. Do not boil as it will curdle the yolks and ruin the texture of the ice cream.

10. Remove from the heat and strain the sauce through a fine sieve into a clean bowl. Add the Amaretto and leave to cool. When cold, churn in an ice-cream machine. Reserve in the freezer.

11. *Strawberry sauce* Place the strawberries in a liquidiser, add the sugar, and liquidise to a smooth pulp. Strain through a fine-mesh sieve into a clean bowl. Discard the seeds. If the sauce is too thick, it can be thinned down with a little of the syrup from the peaches. Chill until needed.

12. *Nougatine* Heat the caster sugar and the glucose syrup together, and caramelise to a golden brown. Immediately add the almonds and butter, and stir together until well mixed. Remove from the heat and transfer to a lightly oiled tray. Using a palette knife spread the nougatine as thinly as possible whilst still warm. Leave to cool. When cold break into pieces (and store in an airtight jar if making in advance).

13. Place the nougatine in a plastic bag and crush with a rolling pin. Place the crushed nougatine on a shallow tray.

14. Take the almond ice cream from the freezer, scoop out six balls of ice cream and roll them in the nougatine.

15. Place the ice cream (both the bulk of it, and the six balls) back in the freezer.

16. *Spun sugar* Mix the caster sugar, glucose syrup and water, and boil until the mixture becomes a golden brown. Remove from the heat and dip the base of the saucepan into a bowl of cold water to stop further cooking.

17. Leave the caramel to cool slightly then dip a fork into it and flick the trailing caramel over a rolling pin. Carefully make a loose ball of spun sugar. Repeat until you have six balls in total. Lay them on a tray. This process must not be done too far in advance as the sugar will collapse.

18. *To serve* Lay out six plates. Spoon the strawberry sauce on to each plate and place a galette in the centre. Place a ball of ice cream on top of the galette and gently press two peach halves together around the ice cream. Place a sprig of mint on top of the peach. Finally top with the prepared spun sugar and sprinkle a little crushed nougatine over the top. Serve immediately. (*Chef's Note:* Make sure it's not your turn to clean the kitchen after preparing the spun sugar!)

Caramelised Apple Tart with Vanilla Ice Cream, Caramel Sauce

You can make the pastry, ice cream and sauce in advance.

---

1 portion

40 g (1½ oz) Puff Pastry (basic 66)
2 apples
½ tablespoon caster sugar
15 g (½ oz) unsalted butter, melted
a little Grand Marnier

Garnishes
1 portion Vanilla Ice Cream (basic 73)
2 tablespoons Caramel Sauce (basic 70)

---

1. Roll the pastry out very thinly and then prick it all over with a fork. You don't want it to rise. Place on a baking sheet, and position a small side plate on top. Cut round to make a fair-sized circle of pastry. Turn over a little at the edges to give an even appearance.
2. Peel, core and halve the apples vertically. Very, very thinly slice them crossways. Fan these slices carefully out around the puff pastry circle, with a few in the middle.
3. Sprinkle with the sugar and pour the melted butter over evenly.
4. Bake in the oven preheated to 180°C/350°F/Gas 4 for 20 minutes. Turn the whole tart over and cook, apple side down, for a further 10 minutes.
5. Bring out of the oven and press flat with the bottom of a pan. Turn right side up and place on a plate.
6. Serve with a scoop of cold ice cream in the middle and warm sauce around.

Tarte Tatin of Pears

Make the pastry well in advance.

---

2 portions

2-3 firm pears, depending on
    size
100 g (4 oz) unsalted butter

100 g (4 oz) caster sugar
100 g (4 oz) Puff Pastry
    (basic 66)

---

1. Peel the pears, cut them in half lengthways, and scoop out the cores.

2. Have ready a round heatproof and ovenproof pan, 15 cm (6 in) in diameter and 5 cm (2 in) deep (preferably copper, and stainless-steel or tin lined). Smooth the butter evenly over it, and sprinkle with the sugar.

3. Place the pear halves, rounded sides down, and thin ends to the middle, around the inside of the pan. You may need 4 or 5 halves of pear.

4. Roll the puff pastry out to a thickness of about 3 mm (1/8 in). Put the pan on top of the pastry and cut out a circle which will fit the pan, leaving a 1 cm (1/2 in) overlap. Put the pastry circle on top of the pears in the pan, and tuck down between pan and pears.

5. Place the pan on top of the stove and heat until the sugar starts to bubble up the sides, caramelise and turn colour.

6. When it reaches a lightish dark brown, place the pan in the oven preheated to 180°C/350°F/Gas 4, and bake until the pastry is cooked and quite firm, about 30 minutes.

7. Remove from the oven and let rest for at least an hour for the flavours of the pear juices and the caramel to amalgamate.

8. To serve, place the pan on a high heat on the stove until the caramel starts to bubble. Shake the pan carefully so that the pastry comes away from the sides of the pan, then quickly turn it upside down on to a serving plate.

9. Cut in half, and serve with fresh double cream.

Millefeuilles of Red Fruits, Sabayon of Kirsch

The pastry can be made in advance and indeed baked in advance, and just gently heated while the fruits are warming and the sabayon – a last-minute sauce – is being completed.

4 portions

200 g (7 oz) Puff Pastry (basic 66)	**Raspberry Coulis (basic 68)**
icing sugar to dust	**1 punnet each of raspberries, blackberries,**
Sweet Sabayon made with Kirsch (basic 71)	**blueberries and redcurrants**

1. Roll the puff pastry out to 3 mm (1/8 in) thickness, and leave to rest in the fridge for an hour. Cut into eight 10 cm (4 in) circles, and put these back in the fridge to rest.

2. Preheat the oven to 220°C/425°F/Gas 7. Place the pastry circles on a non-stick tray and dust with icing sugar. Cook in the oven for about 15 minutes, or until golden brown and shiny on the top. They rise like little balls, with the sugar glazing their tops.

3. Remove from the oven and keep the best of the eight circles for the tops of the millefeuilles. Cut a circle from the bottoms of these and remove any raw pastry from the inside. Do the same at the tops of the other four circles of pastry. Place the tops on the bottoms so you have four double millefeuilles.

4. Make the sabayon, and continue whisking it for 15 minutes.

5. A few minutes before the sabayon is finished, put the raspberry coulis and the red fruit in a pan and heat very, very gently. They should not cook, just warm through.

6. Put one millefeuille in the centre of each plate. Take the top piece off and fill the base piece with fruit and juices, allowing them to spill over and around the edges of the plate. Pour over 2-3 tablespoons of the thick creamy sabayon and top with the glazed puff pastry lid. Serve.

Feuillantine of Raspberries

The pastry can be made and cooled in advance.

It is rolled in this less traditional way, because we want the taste and crisp texture – we do not want it to rise.

---

4 portions

about 700 g (1½ lb) Puff Pastry (basic 66)
icing sugar
600 g (1¼ lb) raspberries

Raspberry Coulis (optional, basic 68)
4 sprigs fresh mint
120 ml (4 fl oz) double cream (optional)

---

1. Roll the puff pastry out on a work surface sprinkled with icing sugar to a rectangle 3 mm (⅛ in) thick. Roll the pastry up like a Swiss roll, and refrigerate for 2 hours.

2. Slice the puff pastry roll into pieces 1 cm (½ in) thick, then roll out each slice until paper thin. Cut into tidy circles using a plain 10 cm (4 in) cutter.

3. Place on a non-stick baking tray and bake in the oven preheated to 200°C/400°F/Gas 6 for about 15 minutes, or until golden brown.

4. Remove from the oven, and turn the circles over. Flatten each with a bang from the bottom of a small saucepan.

5. If the raspberries are good quality, you don't need to coat them with the coulis. If less than the best, swirl the raspberries round in the coulis to glaze them.

6. Build up layers on a plate: first pastry, then raspberries, then pastry and raspberries, finishing with a third piece of pastry. Dust this with icing sugar. Spoon the raspberry coulis around the plate, and top with a couple of raspberries and the mint. If you like, pour the thin cream over the top of the pastry, allowing it to cascade down the sides.

Tarte à l'Orange

Gordon Ramsay, Aubergine, London

Gordon worked his way through my kitchen for going on three years, until I sent him to Le Gavroche and then France. Now he's his own man at Aubergine, and I predict he'll soon get his first Michelin star.

---

8 portions

500 g (18 oz) Sweet Pastry
(basic 78)
1 litre (1¾ pints) fresh
orange juice
400 g (14 oz) caster sugar

9 eggs
freshly grated zest of 4
oranges
250 ml (8 fl oz) double cream

---

1. Roll out the pastry to 5 mm (¼ in) thick, and use to line a 20 cm (8 in) tart ring on a baking sheet, or a tin with a removable base. The ring or tin should be 3.75 cm (1½ in) deep. Do not cut off excess pastry at the top at this stage.
2. Rest for at least an hour in the fridge to ensure the pastry will not shrink, then bake blind – lined with greaseproof paper or foil and baking beans – in the oven preheated to 180°C/350°F/Gas 4 for about 15 minutes, or until all visible pastry is thoroughly cooked. Remove the foil or paper and beans, leave to settle for a moment or two, then continue cooking for about 5 minutes more, until nice and golden. Keep in the ring. Reduce the oven temperature to 130°C/260°F/Gas ½-1.
3. Meanwhile, reduce the orange juice to 250 ml (8 fl oz). This intensifies its flavour. Cool.
4. Whisk the sugar and eggs together thoroughly in a bowl, then add the cool reduced orange juice and the zest. Stir in the cream.
5. Check that the tart base has no holes (if it has, seal with a little raw pastry). Pour in the orange mixture, and cook the tart in the oven for about 35 minutes, or until completely set.
6. Remove from the oven, and cut around the top of the tart, removing all the excess pastry. Let the tart rest for an hour to set. Serve at room temperature.

Prune and Armagnac Tarts

At The Canteen we make individual 10 cm (4 in) tarts, but you could of course make one large tart (see Tarte à l'Orange).

6-8 portions

500 g (18 oz) Sweet Pastry (basic 78)
6 egg yolks
75 g (3 oz) caster sugar
450 ml (15 fl oz) double cream
50 ml (2 fl oz) milk
2 vanilla pods, split
1 teaspoon vanilla essence
150 g (5 oz) Marinated Prunes (basic 76)

Garnishes
12-16 Marinated Prunes (basic 76) and some of their syrup
Armagnac Crème Anglaise (basic 69)
icing sugar

1. Make the sweet pastry as described on page 167, then roll out and use to line six to eight 10 x 1 cm (4 x ½ in) tart rings (or one large ring). Blind-bake as described in Tarte à l'Orange (see page 101).

2. Mix the egg yolks and sugar thoroughly together first, then add the cream and milk, scraped-out vanilla seeds and vanilla essence.

3. Chop the marinated prunes finely and add to the mixture. If possible, keep for a day, chilled, so that the prune flavour thoroughly permeates the milk and the cream.

4. Take some of the chopped prune out of the mixture, and arrange evenly in the centre of each pastry case. Ladle the mixture in on top until full.

5. Bake in the oven preheated to 100°C/220°F/at the very lowest gas, for 30 minutes until completely set. If the oven is too hot, the eggs will scramble and split the mixture.

6. Remove from the oven and leave to rest and set for about an hour.

7. Trim the pastry and remove the rings. Place a small tart in the centre of each plate.

8. Put the prunes and some of their syrup into a small pan and boil to reduce the liquid to a thick syrup.

9. Surround the tart on each plate with the Armagnac sauce. Place the two garnish prunes at the bottom, and spoon a thin line of their reduced dark syrup over the top of the pale sauce for a nice effect. Sprinkle with icing sugar and serve warm.

Tarte au Citron

A lemon tart cannot be served straightaway, as the middle will still be quite wet and runny. It needs to rest and set for at least an hour, when it will still be warm – the best way to serve it. However, it also tastes good cold a day later.

---

8 portions

500 g (18 oz) Sweet Pastry (basic 78)	9 eggs
	390 g (13½ oz) caster sugar
5 lemons	250 ml (8 fl oz) double cream

---

1. Make the sweet pastry as described on page 167, then roll, line and blind-bake as in the previous recipe. Check that there are no holes in the pastry case.

2. Finely grate the zest from four of the lemons, and squeeze the juice from them all.

3. Whisk the eggs and sugar together thoroughly in a bowl, then add the lemon juice and zest. Stir in the cream.

4. Pour the lemon mixture into the pastry case and cook in the oven preheated to 130°C/260°F/Gas ½-1 for 30-40 minutes, until starting to set in the centre.

5. Remove from the oven, and trim and rest as for the previous recipe.

TIP

This lemon tart is served in The Restaurant with a frozen parfait ice cream called chiboust, and a small lemon soufflé as an Assiette Citron.

Tarte aux Poires Quatres Epices

Philippe Dadé

Philippe is an old mate, one of the best pâtissiers in Britain. He also makes fantastic bread. He supports me, helps me, encourages me – we're more like brothers in many ways.

---

8 portions

3-5 pears, depending on size
1 x 20 cm (8 in) Sweet Pastry flan case (made and blind-baked as on page 101)
apricot jam to glaze (optional)

Syrup
1 litre (1¾ pints) water
350 g (12 oz) granulated sugar
30 g (1¼ oz) star anise
6 cinnamon sticks
8 vanilla pods, split

15 g (½ oz) finely grated fresh ginger

Frangipane
250 ml (8 fl oz) syrup (made from 120 g/4 oz caster sugar and 120 ml/4 fl oz water)
250 ml (8 fl oz) pear syrup quatre épices (see above), strained
16 egg yolks
75 g (3 oz) caster sugar
50 g (2 oz) dried milk powder
20 g (¾ oz) plain flour

---

1. Put the syrup ingredients in a heavy-based pan and bring to the boil. Leave to infuse for 1 hour.

2. Peel the pears, cut them into halves, and core. Poach them in the syrup until they are still slightly hard to the touch. Leave in the syrup to cool.

3. To make the frangipane, put the two syrups into a pan and bring to the boil.

4. Whisk the yolks, sugar and milk powder together.

5. Pour one-third of the hot syrup into the yolk mixture, and mix in, along with the flour.

6. Pour this back into the pan containing the bulk of the boiling syrup. Cook gently until it comes back to the boil, stirring constantly.

7. Pour into the tart case to come three-quarters up the height of the case. Arrange the pear halves, flat side down, around the tart and cook in the oven preheated to 160°C/325°F/Gas 3 for about 30 minutes or until the pastry is golden brown and the filling is set.

8. Remove from the oven and leave to get cold. Glaze with apricot jam if you like.

Sablé of Pears with Red Fruit

The sablé must be made at least 12 hours in advance, but will keep well raw for a day.

You can freeze the raw dough: roll it up into a cylinder, and slice off what you need.

Baked, the sablé biscuits will keep for a couple of days in an airtight tin.

The pears can be poached a couple of days in advance.

6 portions

about 6 medium pears, peeled
Poaching Syrup to cover (basic 67)
Poire William
2 vanilla pods
about 4 punnets mixed fresh 'red' summer fruit, prepared (1 each, say, of raspberries, blueberries, redcurrants, blackberries)
85 ml (3 fl oz) Raspberry Coulis (optional, basic 68)

Sweet Sabayon (basic 71)
icing sugar
6 sprigs fresh mint

Sablé
400 g (14 oz) unsalted butter, softened
200 g (7 oz) caster sugar
1 egg yolk
500 g (18 oz) plain flour

1. To make the sablé, cream the soft butter and sugar together by hand in a rounded bowl. Add the egg yolk and mix in lightly, then add the flour. Mix in with the fingers to a nice crumb texture.

2. Place on a working surface, preferably marble, and rub together, then roll into a ball. Wrap in cling film, and leave to rest and set in the fridge for at least 12 hours.

3. Roll out to about 3 mm (⅛ in) thick and cut into rectangles of 7.5 x 5 cm (3 x 2 in). Rest these for another hour in the fridge.

4. Bake in the oven preheated to 170°C/340°F/Gas 3-4 until light golden brown, about 10-12 minutes. Be careful, as the taste changes quite dramatically the darker the sablé becomes.

5. Poach the pears until tender in syrup to cover, with the Poire William (50 ml/2 fl oz per 500 ml/17 fl oz syrup) and the split vanilla pods. Test to see if they are ready with a thin knife: the knife blade should meet a little bite or resistance in the centre. Leave to cool in the syrup, then chill. Halve and core.

6. If you like, roll the red fruits in the raspberry coulis to give them a red glaze. Make the sweet sabayon at the last minute.

7. To serve, place a layer of sablé in the centre of each plate and top with a half pear, sliced and fanned out. Coat with a little sabayon. Repeat this with another layer of sablé, a half pear and more sabayon. Top with a third sablé biscuit, and sprinkle with icing sugar, a small amount of the red fruit, and the mint. Arrange the remaining red fruits around the plate.

Pavé de Chocolat

You could make the sponge and the mousses a day in advance.

---

12 portions

Chocolate sponge
6 eggs, separated
caster sugar
165 g (5½ oz) plain flour
100 g (4 oz) cornflour
25 g (1 oz) cocoa powder
**300 ml (10 fl oz) syrup, made
   with 150 ml (5 fl oz) water
   and 150 g (5 oz) caster sugar**
about 2 tablespoons dark rum

Dark chocolate mousse
**400 g (14 oz) good dark
   chocolate**

12 egg yolks
250 g (9 oz) caster sugar
**150 ml (5 fl oz) espresso
   coffee**
**700 ml (1⅕ pints) double
   cream**

White chocolate mousse
**300 g (11 oz) good white
   chocolate**
3 gelatine leaves
85 ml (3 fl oz) hot water
**300 ml (10 fl oz) double
   cream**

---

1. *Chocolate sponge* Whip together the egg yolks and 75 g (3 oz) caster sugar. In a separate bowl whip the egg whites and 100 g (4 oz) sugar until stiff.

2. Sieve together the flours and the cocoa powder.

3. Pour the egg yolk mixture into the egg whites. Add the dry mixture slowly and fold all together very carefully. You don't want the egg white to lose its volume.

4. Spread the mixture carefully on to a non-stick 60 x 40 cm (24 x 16 in) tray. Bake in the oven preheated to 180-190°C/350-375°F/Gas 4-5 for about 20 minutes. To test that it is ready, poke in the middle with a finger: if the indentation stays for a couple of seconds before bouncing back, the sponge is ready. Cool in the tray on a wire rack.

5. When cool, moisten with syrup mixed with rum.

6. *Dark chocolate mousse* Break the chocolate into small pieces and melt slowly in a bowl over a pan of hot water.

7. Place the egg yolks in a bowl and beat together well. Place over a pan of hot water or in a bain-marie.

8. Make a syrup with the sugar and espresso coffee, and pour this on to the egg yolks, whisking continuously until cold.

9. When cold, mix this sabayon with the melted chocolate and then the whipped cream. Leave to cool.

10. Spread this dark chocolate mousse over the moistened sponge base. Place in the fridge to set.

11. *White chocolate mousse* Break the white chocolate into small pieces and melt slowly in a bowl over a pan of hot water.

12. Put the gelatine leaves in the hot water and warm a little to melt.

13. Mix the gelatine and melted chocolate, then fold in the whipped cream.

14. Spread this evenly and smoothly on top of the set dark chocolate mousse. Bang the tray to ensure there are no air bubbles. Put in the fridge to set – this takes quite a time.

15. Cut the layered *pavé* into twelve (or more, or less, portions), and serve simply by itself, or with some cream.

Cadeau de Chocolat

1. Simply melt some dark chocolate as on page 109.

2. Measure the diameter of the individual *pavé* – about 15 cm (6 in) say – and cut a strip of pliable plastic of about 18 cm (7 in) long by 10-13 cm (4-5 in) wide.

3. Spread the melted chocolate on to one side of the plastic strip using a palette knife.

4. Gripping the strip on either side with your fingertips, lift it up and wrap it around your *pavé*. Crimp it in slowly with your fingers at the top so that it comes over the top and wraps the *pavé* like a parcel. Place in the fridge to set.

5. Once set, bring out and slowly start to take off the plastic outside with your nails. It will come off in one piece, and will leave a shimmer on the chocolate which looks almost metallic. You are left with a chocolate-wrapped gift box of chocolate!

TIP

You could serve this with a Crème Anglaise (basic 69), flavoured with cinnamon.

BASIC RECIPES

Basic 1
Chicken Stock

We use this 'single-cooked' chicken stock in juice-based sauces.

Makes about 4.5 litres (8 pints)

2.75 kg (6 lb) raw chicken carcasses, chopped	1 leek
about 5.75 litres (10 pints) cold water	1 large onion
3 celery stalks	2 carrots
	1/2 whole head of garlic

---

1. Place the raw chicken carcasses in a large pot, then cover with cold water. Bring to the boil, then skim.

2. Keep the vegetables whole, but peel them if necessary. Tie the celery and leek together with string – this prevents them breaking up, and this helps to clarify the stock.

3. Add all the vegetables and the garlic to the pot, then bring back to the boil. Skim and simmer for 4 hours.

4. Pass through a fine sieve. The stock should be a light amber colour, and clear. Store in the fridge for a couple of days, or freeze (but for no longer than three months).

TIP

Use this recipe as a basis for other poultry stocks – with duck, guinea fowl etc.

Basic 2
Double Chicken Stock

We use this 'twice-cooked' chicken stock in cream-based sauces, where it compensates for the diminution of flavour.

Makes about 1 litre (1³/₄ pints)

900 g (2 lb) chicken winglets	**¹/₂ whole head of garlic**
2 tablespoons olive oil	**1.5 litres (2¹/₂ pints) Chicken**
1 large carrot, chopped	**Stock (basic 1)**
1 celery stalk, chopped	**1 bay leaf**
¹/₂ large onion	**1 sprig fresh thyme**
the white of 1 leek	**3 sprigs fresh parsley**

1. Chop each winglet into three or four pieces and cook half of them in half of the oil, without colouring.

2. Peel and trim the vegetables as appropriate. Cut into small dice (*mirepoix*). Peel and finely chop the garlic.

3. Separately cook the *mirepoix* vegetables, plus the garlic, in the remaining oil, without colouring.

4. Add the *mirepoix* to the cooked winglets, add the raw winglets, then cover with the chicken stock. Bring to the boil and skim. (Adding the raw winglets helps to clarify the stock.)

5. Add the bay leaf, thyme and parsley and simmer for about 1 hour.

6. Pass through a fine sieve lined with muslin. The stock should be an amber colour. Keep in the fridge for up to a week, or freeze (but for no longer than three months).

Basic 3
Veal Stock

Veal stock, the bane of domestic cooks and the mainstay of professional cooks, is used primarily because it gives a sauce so much more body – because of the gelatine in the bones used. It brings a sauce together. You can, of course, halve the recipe.

Makes about 3 litres (5¼ pints)

2.75 kg (6 lb) veal knuckle bones	450 g (1 lb) button mushrooms, thinly sliced
120 ml (4 fl oz) olive oil	¼ bottle Madeira
1 onion, chopped	10 litres (17½ pints) hot water
3 carrots, chopped	
3 celery stalks, chopped	1 sprig fresh thyme
½ whole head of garlic	1 bay leaf
4 tablespoons tomato purée	

1. Cook the veal knuckle bones in 4 tablespoons of the oil until golden brown, stirring and turning occasionally.

2. Simultaneously, in a separate pan, cook the onion, carrot, celery, and garlic in 2 tablespoons of the oil until golden brown, without burning.

3. Add the tomato purée to the vegetables, stir in and allow to gently and lightly colour. Be careful not to burn at this stage.

4. In a separate pan, colour the button mushrooms in the remaining oil, then deglaze with the Madeira. Boil to reduce down to almost nothing. Add the syrupy mushrooms to the rest of the vegetables.

5. When the veal bones are golden brown, place in a large stock pot and cover with the hot water. Bring to the boil and skim.

6. Add the vegetables and herbs to the bones and bring back to the boil. Skim, then allow to simmer for 8-12 hours, topping up with water to keep the bones covered as and when required.

7. Pass through a fine sieve into another, preferably tall, pan, and boil to reduce by half. Cool, then store in the fridge for up to a week, or freeze (but for no longer than three months).

Basic 4
Lamb Stock/Sauce

To make a sauce from the stock below, allow about 120-150 ml (4-5 fl oz) per person. Place in a small saucepan and boil to reduce by half. Add a sprig of a herb relevant to the dish being prepared, and leave to infuse for 10 minutes or so. Then heat through briefly, add a small knob of butter and season to taste with salt and pepper. Strain.

Makes about 1.5 litres (2½ pints)

2.25 kg (5 lb) raw lamb bones	1 whole head of garlic
2 tablespoons vegetable oil	1.5 litres (2½ pints) Veal
1 onion	Stock (basic 3)
1 celery stalk	1 litre (1¾ pints) Chicken
1 carrot	Stock (basic 1)
1 leek	500 ml (17 fl oz) water
2½ tablespoons Tomato	1 bay leaf
Fondue (basic 34)	1 sprig fresh thyme

1. Chop the lamb bones very finely, then roast them in 1 tablespoon of the oil in a tray on top of the stove until golden brown. Drain well.

2. Prepare the vegetables as appropriate, then cut into dice. Sweat in the remaining oil on top of the stove. Do not colour them.

3. Add the tomato fondue and the peeled garlic cloves, and cook right down to a 'jam'. Add the lamb bones.

4. Bring the two stocks to the boil in a separate pan, and pour over the bones to cover. Bring back to the boil and add the cold water. This coagulates the fat in the stock, and it will rise to the top. Skim off thoroughly.

5. Add the herbs and cook the stock at a fast simmer for 1 hour, skimming regularly. It will reduce down to about 1.5 litres (2½ pints).

6. Pass through a sieve, then through muslin six times to ensure that it is clear. Cool and store, or freeze, or use in a sauce (see above).

Basic 5
Pigeon Stock/Sauce

To make a sauce from the stock below, do the same as for the lamb stock on page 116. Infuse with thyme flowers, and finish off with a knob of foie gras butter (Basic 60).

Makes about 1 litre (1¾ pints)

carcasses of 4 pigeons, including the winglets, neck and feet
2 tablespoons vegetable oil
2 shallots
1 carrot
1 celery stalk
3-4 mushrooms
1 whole head of garlic
3-4 juniper berries, crushed
2 tablespoons Tomato Fondue (basic 34)

1 tablespoon white wine
1 tablespoon each of Armagnac and Madeira
1 litre (1¾ pints) Veal Stock (basic 3)
1 litre (1¾ pints) Chicken Stock (basic 1)
1 bay leaf
1 sprig fresh thyme
livers and hearts of 4 pigeons

---

1. Chop the carcasses and trimmings very finely and roast in a tray in 1 tablespoon of the oil on top of the stove until golden brown. Drain well.

2. Prepare the vegetables as appropriate, then cut into dice. Sweat in the remaining oil on top of the stove, along with the peeled garlic cloves and juniper berries. Do not colour.

3. Add the tomato fondue, and cook right down to a 'jam'.

4. Add the chopped carcasses and deglaze first with the white wine. Do the same with the Armagnac and Madeira.

5. Add the stocks, and bring to the boil. Skim well, then add the herbs, pigeon livers and hearts, and cook at a fast simmer for 20 minutes. It will reduce down to about 1 litre (1¾ pints).

6. Pass through a sieve, then through muslin six times, to ensure that it is clear. Cool and store, or freeze, or use in a sauce (see above).

WILD FOOD FROM LAND AND SEA

Basic 6
Madeira Jelly

This makes a very flavourful jelly to accompany the terrine of foie gras on pages 36–7, but it can also be used as a consommé or broth.

Do not reduce, as you would for the jelly, then to the hot broth add herbs, wild mushrooms or vegetable dice to taste.

Make the full amount – I know it's a lot, and extravagant – and freeze the bulk for later use.

Makes about 3 litres (5¼ pints)

1 shin of veal, chopped into *osso buco*	2 celery stalks
1 shin of beef, cut similarly	2 leeks
1 boiling fowl, chopped into small joints	1 head of garlic, cut in half
1 calf's foot, split	1 bouquet garni
2 onions, with skins	1 bottle Madeira
2 large carrots, split lengthways	500 ml (17 fl oz) soy sauce
	10 litres (17½ pints) water

---

1. Put the meats into a large stock pot along with all the remaining ingredients, and bring to the boil.
2. Skim very well, and then cook, uncovered, for 2½ hours. The liquid must barely simmer, so that it doesn't go cloudy.
3. Pass gently through muslin into another pan: the liquid should be totally clear and amber in colour, and can now be used for a broth or consommé. It will not need salt, because of the soy.
4. Reduce by half by simmering for the jelly. It will be intensely flavoured. Leave to set in one or two shallow trays, then chop finely and pipe or spoon for decoration.

Basic 7
Fish Stock

The best bones to use are turbot or Dover sole, although monkfish is good too.

Use the stock for poaching fish, or in fish sauces or soups.

Makes about 2 litres (3½ pints)

1.8 kg (4 lb) fish bones
white of 1 small leek, finely
   chopped
1 large celery stalk, finely
   chopped
½ onion, finely chopped
½ fennel bulb, finely
   chopped

½ whole head of garlic,
   sliced horizontally
1 tablespoon olive oil
200 ml (7 fl oz) white wine
2 litres (3½ pints) water
1 lemon, sliced
2 sprigs fresh parsley

---

1. Wash the fish bones very thoroughly, and chop up.
2. Cook the vegetables and garlic in the oil for a few minutes to soften, without colouring.
3. Add the fish bones and white wine and cook, without colouring (the bones will turn white), for about 5 more minutes, then reduce the wine a little.
4. Add the water, bring to the boil and skim well.
5. Add the sliced lemon and parsley, then simmer for 20 minutes.
6. Pass through a sieve and leave to cool. Store in the fridge for a day only, or freeze (but for no longer than a month).

Basic 8
Scallop Stock

A stock made from scallop trimmings always makes the best sauce for scallops. Never throw scallop skirts away as they are so full of flavour that can be utilised in a stock.

To make into a sauce, reduce 150 ml (5 fl oz) stock per person by half, then add 1 tablespoon double cream, a teaspoon unsalted butter, and lemon juice, salt and pepper to taste. Whisk up with a little hand blender.

Makes about 2 litres (3¹/₂ pints)

18 scallop skirts, well cleaned	1 tablespoon olive oil
1 carrot, finely chopped	2 litres (3¹/₂ pints) Fish Stock (basic 7), or water
1 celery stalk, finely chopped	1 cinnamon stick
1 small leek, finely chopped	zest of 1 lemon

---

1. Cook the vegetables in the oil for a few minutes to soften, without colouring.

2. Add the scallop skirts and cook for a few minutes more, without colouring.

3. Add the fish stock or water, bring to the boil and skim.

4. Add the cinnamon and lemon zest and cook for 20 minutes (any longer, and the cinnamon and lemon will turn bitter).

5. Pass through a muslin-lined sieve, and leave to cool. Store in the fridge for about a day, or freeze (but for no longer than a month).

TIP

Always get your fishmonger to trim and clean fish and shellfish, but take the trimmings home with you and use to make a stock or sauce (or freeze for future use). When cooking shellfish, keep their poaching liquor and add to a fish stock – for instance clam and mussel liquor added to fish stock makes a good stock for the soup on page 23.

Basic 9
Jus de Nage

Use this for poaching fish or shellfish, or in delicate fish sauces. It's handy to have for when you might like to let a velouté down. It's nicely aniseedy in flavour.

Makes about 2 litres (3½ pints)

2 onions, coarsely chopped
1 leek, coarsely chopped
2 celery stalks, coarsely chopped
5 carrots, coarsely chopped
1 whole head of garlic, sliced horizontally
6 lemon slices
8 white peppercorns
20 pink peppercorns
1 bay leaf
2 star anise
1.75 litres (3 pints) cold water
a sprig each of fresh parsley, coriander, tarragon, thyme and chervil
200 ml (7 fl oz) dry white wine

1. Place all the vegetables in a large pan with the garlic, lemon slices, peppercorns, bay and star anise, then add just enough water to cover.

2. Bring to the boil, then reduce the heat and simmer for 8 minutes. Add the herbs and cook for a further 2 minutes only.

3. Remove the pan from the heat and add the white wine. Pour the mixture into a large bowl or jar, cover and leave to infuse for 1½ days in the fridge.

4. Strain the stock through a muslin-lined sieve and discard all the solids. Store the stock in the fridge for a few days, or freeze (but for no longer than a month).

Basic 10
Court Bouillon

Use this for poaching fish and shellfish. It's particularly good for cooking crabs.

Makes about 1.75 litres (3 pints)

3 leeks, coarsely chopped
1 carrot, coarsely chopped
1 celery stalk, coarsely
  chopped
4 shallots, coarsely chopped
3 onions, coarsely chopped
1 leaf of bulb fennel
a sprig each of fresh thyme
  and tarragon
a few parsley stalks
1 whole head of garlic, sliced
  horizontally
1.75 litres (3 pints) cold
  water
8 white peppercorns
20 g (3/4 oz) salt
zest of 1 lemon
1 star anise
250 ml (8 fl oz) dry white
  wine

---

1. Place all the vegetables and the herbs in a large pan with the head of garlic. Add enough cold water to cover, and bring to the boil.

2. Add the peppercorns, salt, lemon zest, star anise and white wine, then simmer the mixture for 35 minutes.

3. Pass through a sieve and discard the solids. The court bouillon is now ready to use. Store in the fridge for a day, or freeze (but for no longer than a month).

Basic 11
Sauce Bercy

This is a good, honest, red wine sauce, that is very good with the calf's liver on page 71, but also with fillet or entrecôte of beef.

4 portions

10 shallots, finely sliced into
   rings
150 ml (5 fl oz) port
500 ml (17 fl oz) red wine
300 ml (10 fl oz) Veal Stock
   (basic 3)

10 g (¼ oz) unsalted butter
1 teaspoon double cream
salt and freshly ground white
   pepper

1. Marinate the shallots in the port for 24 hours, then cook in the port until soft. Cool in the port, then strain, keeping both.
2. Reduce the port and red wine together by four-fifths, down to about 130 ml (4½ fl oz).
3. Add the veal stock to this reduction and bring to the boil. Boil to reduce to a good sauce consistency.
4. Add the cooked shallots and whisk in the butter along with the cream. Taste and correct seasoning.

Basic 12
Jus of Herbs

This is particularly delicious with the herbed chicken on page 74. It could be made at least a week in advance.

It would also be good with pigeon: replace the chicken stock with pigeon stock.

2 portions

legs and winglets from 1
   free-range chicken
50 ml (2 fl oz) olive oil
2 shallots
1/2 carrot
1 celery stalk
1/2 garlic clove
1/2 white of leek

2 tablespoons Tomato
   Fondue (basic 34)
250 ml (8 fl oz) Double
   Chicken Stock (basic 2)
1 sprig fresh thyme
1/2 bay leaf
1 small sprig each of fresh
   tarragon and parsley

1. Chop the legs and winglets and brown in the oil in a large pan. Remove using a slotted spoon.

2. Trim, peel and roughly chop all the vegetables. Caramelise them in the oil remaining in the chicken pan.

3. Add the tomato fondue to the vegetables, and cook, stirring constantly, to mix all well together.

4. Add the browned bones, the stock and enough water to cover. Bring to the boil, then add the thyme and bay and leave to cook slowly for 20-30 minutes to a lovely golden brown.

5. Pass through a sieve, then boil to reduce the liquid by half.

6. Add the finely chopped tarragon and parsley leaves at the last minute, and allow them to infuse for a few minutes before serving.

Basic 13
Sauce Albufera

This rich sauce is best with poultry, particularly the guinea fowl on page 75.

If some green peppercorns are added, it is good with duck (see page 76).

---

2 portions

400 ml (14 fl oz) Double Chicken Stock (basic 2)	**150 g (5 oz) Foie Gras Butter (basic 60)**
400 ml (14 fl oz) double cream	**salt and freshly ground white pepper**

---

1. Place the stock in a pan and boil to reduce by a third.

2. Add the double cream, bring to the boil, and cook for a few minutes until the sauce thickens enough to coat the back of a spoon.

3. Remove from the heat and add the foie gras butter, allowing it to melt gently and evenly into the sauce.

4. Season with salt and pepper to taste.

WILD FOOD FROM LAND AND SEA

Basic 14
Velouté for Fish

This basic cream sauce for fish is best made on the day, although the reduction could be prepared in advance and frozen. Velouté is a mother sauce of several variations, see below.

4 portions

6 shallots, thinly sliced
15 g (½ oz) unsalted butter
500 ml (17 fl oz) white wine
500 ml (17 fl oz) Noilly Prat

1 litre (1¾ pints) Fish Stock
   (basic 7)
1 litre (1¾ pints) double
   cream

1. Cook the shallots in the butter until softened, without colouring.
2. Deglaze with the white wine and Noilly Prat, and boil to reduce to a syrup.
3. Add the fish stock and boil to reduce by half.
4. Add the cream, bring to the boil and simmer for 5 minutes to reduce to a coating consistency. Pass through a fine sieve. Chill, covered with cling film, if not using immediately.

Basic 15
Sabayon of Grain Mustard

4 portions

400 ml (14 fl oz) Velouté for
   Fish (see above)
4 egg yolks
4 tablespoons warm clarified
   butter

4 teaspoons double cream,
   whipped
2 teaspoons grain mustard

1. Gently beat the egg yolks with a few drops of water in a round-bottomed bowl over a bain-marie. As the egg yolks thicken and cook smoothly, add the warm clarified butter and remove from the heat.
2. Reduce the velouté by half and allow to cool slightly. Add the smooth thickened egg mixture with the whipped cream and the mustard. The texture should be thick but pourable.

126

Basic 16
Tapenade Sauce

Per 50-85 ml (2-3 fl oz) individual portion of Velouté for Fish (see page 126), add and mix in 1 tablespoon Tapenade (basic 37). Finish with 15 g ($1/2$ oz) unsalted butter.

Basic 17
Sauternes Sauce

Another good fish sauce. The reduction could be done in advance, and then frozen. Add the cream later.

8 portions

7 shallots, very finely sliced
7 button mushrooms, very finely sliced
200 g (7 oz) unsalted butter
375 ml (13 fl oz) Sauternes (sweet white wine)
200 ml (7 fl oz) Double Chicken Stock (basic 2)

200 ml (7 fl oz) Fish Stock (basic 7)
300 ml (10 fl oz) double cream
salt and freshly ground white pepper

1. Sweat the shallot and mushrooms in 25 g (1 oz) of the butter until softened, without colouring.
2. Add the Sauternes and boil to reduce by half.
3. Add the double chicken stock and boil to reduce by half.
4. Add the fish stock and boil to reduce by half.
5. Add the double cream and simmer for 2 minutes then pass through a fine sieve into another pan. Return to the stove.
6. Dice the remaining butter and whisk it into the sauce. Season to taste.

Basic 18
Sauce Lie de Vin

Yet another good fish sauce, ideal with salmon, John Dory, red mullet and sea bass. The reduction could be prepared in advance and frozen. Add the cream later.

8 portions

4 shallots, finely sliced
325 g (11½ oz) unsalted butter
1¾ bottles red wine
¼ bottle ruby port
500 ml (17 fl oz) Fish Stock (basic 7)

500 ml (17 fl oz) Veal Stock (basic 3)
1 star anise
100 ml (3½ fl oz) double cream
salt and freshly ground white pepper

1. Sweat the shallots in 25 g (1 oz) of the butter until softened, without colouring.
2. Add the wine and port, and boil to reduce by two-thirds.
3. In another pan boil the fish and veal stocks together with the star anise to reduce by half.
4. Add the stock reduction to the wine and port reduction. Boil together for 5 minutes, then pass through a muslin cloth into yet another pan.
5. Add the cream, and return to the stove. Dice the remaining butter and whisk into the sauce. Season to taste.

Basic 19
Bouillabaisse Sauce

This is not so much a sauce, as it is a soup – the fish soup made with red mullet on pages 22–3. Make the soup as usual then freeze any left over to use as a sauce another time.

Or make the soup in smaller amounts to use as a sauce. Per portion of about 50-85 ml (2-3 fl oz), stir in 1 table-spoon of Rouille 1 (basic 24). Do not boil, as this will ruin the texture.

Basic 20
Hollandaise Sauce

A wonderful classic sauce, to be served with salmon, asparagus etc.

4 portions

3 egg yolks	salt and cayenne pepper
5 tablespoons water	250 g (9 oz) cold unsalted
juice of 1/2 lemon	butter, diced

1. Put the egg yolks, water and lemon juice into a cold saucepan with 1/2 teaspoon salt and a pinch of cayenne. Beat together thoroughly.
2. Add the butter dice to the pan and place over a moderate heat.
3. Whisk while the butter gently melts gradually and evenly into the egg yolks. Continue beating and whisking over mod-erate heat until the sauce thickens.
4. The sauce can be kept warm over a very low heat – or in a bowl over a pan of warm water – for up to 2 hours.

Basic 21
Sauce Choron

A chunky hollandaise which is good with lobster.

4 portions

hollandaise sauce (see page 129)
2 shallots, finely chopped
4 sprigs fresh tarragon, chopped
4 tablespoons white wine or tarragon vinegar

$1/2$ teaspoon white peppercorns
2 tomatoes, skinned, seeded and diced
1 teaspoon good tomato purée

1. Put the shallot, tarragon, vinegar and peppercorns into a small pan, and reduce to a syrup.
2. Strain into the hollandaise, and mix in with the remaining ingredients.

Basic 22
Mustard Beurre Blanc

This sauce is particularly good with smoked haddock (see page 59). Without the mustard, you have a classic beurre blanc.

4 portions

1 teaspoon white wine vinegar
2 teaspoons white wine
2 shallots, very finely chopped
1 teaspoon double cream

250 g (9 oz) cold unsalted butter, diced
1 tablespoon grain mustard
salt and freshly ground white pepper

1. Place the vinegar, wine and shallot in a small pan and reduce to a syrup.
2. Add the cream and reduce a little more.
3. Add the butter dice and whisk in until amalgamated.
4. Stir in the grain mustard and season to taste.

Basic 23
Mayonnaise

A classic recipe with a hint of white heat.

4-6 portions

2 egg yolks
1 tablespoon Dijon mustard
2 tablespoons white wine
   vinegar

1 teaspoon salt
a dash of Tabasco sauce
500 ml (17 fl oz) peanut oil

1. Place the egg yolks, mustard, vinegar, salt and Tabasco in a bowl and mix together until the salt has dissolved.
2. Add the oil in drops at first, whisking in so that the yolks can absorb the oil. When about half the oil has been added, it can be added in slightly larger amounts, but continue whisking.
3. Whisk until all the oil has been added, and the sauce is thick and creamy. Store in the fridge, covered, for up to a week.

Basic 24
Rouille 1

Like a mayonnaise, this and the following recipe can keep for a few days in the fridge, covered with cling film. This is the rouille to add to the bouillabaisse sauce on page 129. Use 1 tablespoon per portion of sauce.

Makes about 300 ml (10 fl oz)

2 egg yolks
1 teaspoon tomato purée
1 pinch saffron strands
120 ml (4 fl oz) olive oil

120 ml (4 fl oz) peanut oil
salt and freshly ground white
   pepper

1. Place the egg yolks in a bowl and mix in the tomato purée and saffron.
2. Mix the oils together, then start adding slowly as for a mayonnaise. Beat in gradually until thick.
3. Taste and season.

Basic 25
Rouille 2

Use this rouille to garnish the fish soup on pages 22–3.

Makes about 300 ml (10 fl oz)

2 egg yolks
50 g (2 oz) cooked potato, puréed
1 hard-boiled egg yolk, sieved

2 pinches saffron strands
2 garlic cloves, crushed
200 ml (7 fl oz) olive oil
salt

---

1. Place the egg yolks, potato, egg, saffron and garlic in a bowl and mix together.
2. Add the oil slowly as for a mayonnaise. Beat in gradually until thick.
3. Taste and season.

Basic 26
Sauce Vierge

This is a wonderful sauce, fresh and more-ish. It's best with fish and shellfish.

---

4 portions

85 ml (3 fl oz) olive oil
25 ml (1 fl oz) lemon juice
1 teaspoon coriander seeds, crushed

8 basil leaves, cut into strips (*julienne*)
2 tomatoes, skinned, seeded and diced

---

1. Heat the oil gently in a small pan, then add the lemon juice. Remove from the heat.
2. Add the coriander and basil, and leave to infuse in the warm oil for a few minutes.
3. Add the tomato dice and serve immediately.

Basic 27
Sauce Antiboise

Another wonderful fresh sauce, great with grilled fish.

4 portions

2 shallots, very finely chopped
1 garlic clove, crushed
120 ml (4 fl oz) olive oil
8 basil leaves, cut into fine strips (*julienne*)

12 coriander leaves, cut into fine strips
2 medium tomatoes, skinned, seeded and diced
salt and freshly ground white pepper
2 drops lemon juice

1. Cook the shallot and garlic in the oil without colouring.
2. Add the herbs and leave for a few minutes to infuse with the oil.
3. Add the tomatoes to warm them through only, then season with salt and pepper and a little lemon juice.

Basic 28
Sauce Gribiche

This cold sauce will last a couple of days in the fridge.

10 portions

4 hard-boiled eggs, shelled
the same weight each of capers and small gherkins (*cornichons*)

1 tablespoon chopped fresh tarragon
3 tablespoons chopped fresh parsley
4-5 tablespoons olive oil

1. Weigh the eggs out of their shells, and then measure out the same weight of both capers and gherkins.
2. Separate the yolks from the whites; sieve the yolks and finely chop the whites. Chop the capers and gherkins. Mix all together in a bowl.
3. Add the fresh chopped herbs to the bowl, and then pour in 4 tablespoons of the oil gradually, mixing just to bind. You may need a little more oil, but the texture should be of a nice paste, not runny.

Basic 29
Vinaigrette 1

This keeps well for up to a week.

Makes 400 ml (14 fl oz)

75 ml (2³/₄ fl oz) white wine
  vinegar
salt and freshly ground white
  pepper

120 ml (4 fl oz) peanut oil
200 ml (7 fl oz) olive oil

---

1. Place the vinegar in a bowl and add a pinch each of salt and pepper. Stir to dissolve.
2. Add the oils and whisk to an emulsion. Taste and adjust seasoning if necessary. Store in a suitable container.

Basic 30
Vinaigrette 2

A good dressing for a salad of leaves, or the tian on pages 28–9.

Makes 400 ml (14 fl oz)

50 ml (2 fl oz) red wine
50 ml (2 fl oz) sherry vinegar
salt and freshly ground white
  pepper

250 ml (8 fl oz) peanut oil
50 ml (2 fl oz) olive oil

Make, mix and store as in the previous recipe.

Basic 31
Water Vinaigrette

This is a different type of vinaigrette. You don't want to create an emulsion, but a mottled effect on the plate: it's a very clear and light dressing. Make it in the quantities you desire: with teaspoons, tablespoons, bottle caps etc.

---

1 part white wine vinegar
5 parts water
8 parts olive oil
1 garlic clove, crushed

1 sprig fresh tarragon
salt and freshly ground white
  pepper

---

1. Mix the liquids together.
2. Add the garlic and tarragon, and infuse for an hour or so before straining. Season to taste.

Basic 32
Truffle Vinaigrette

We make our own truffle juice at The Restaurant – an intense essence of truffle – but you can buy it in good specialist shops.

Makes 600 ml (1 pint)

50 ml (2 fl oz) truffle juice
50 ml (2 fl oz) sherry vinegar
500 ml (17 fl oz) peanut oil

salt and freshly ground white
  pepper

Mix together as you would any vinaigrette, and season to taste.

Basic 33
Tomato Coulis

This is best made fresh. It's a useful sauce.

4 portions

200 g (7 oz) good tomatoes, roughly chopped
50 ml (2 fl oz) red wine vinegar
40 g (1½ oz) tomato purée
a dash each of Tabasco and tomato ketchup

salt and freshly ground white pepper
50 ml (2 fl oz) extra virgin olive oil

1. Place all the ingredients except the oil in a processor and blend to a purée.
2. Add the oil and blend for 30 seconds
3. Pass three times through a fine strainer to make it nice and smooth.

Basic 34
Tomato Fondue

This is like a fresh tomato sauce, which is useful in a number of recipes. It could be made a couple of days in advance.

Makes about 150 ml (5 fl oz)

6-8 large ripe plum tomatoes
100 ml (3½ fl oz) olive oil
½ shallot, finely chopped
1 garlic clove, finely chopped

1 sprig fresh thyme
¼ bay leaf

1. Blanch the tomatoes in boiling water for about 30 seconds, then remove and discard skin and seeds. Chop the flesh into small dice.

2. Heat the olive oil in a pan and sweat the shallot and garlic for a few minutes without colouring. Add the tomato dice and thyme. Cook very gently until all the moisture has been removed from the tomato, and you are left with a dry tomato paste.

3. Remove the sprig of thyme and put the mixture in the blender. Blend until smooth.

Basic 35
Pistou

This is good on soups, or as a pasta sauce.

Makes about 350 ml (12 fl oz)

50 g (2 oz) pine kernels
50 g (2 oz) garlic cloves, peeled
50 g (2 oz) Parmesan cheese, finely grated

30 basil leaves
200 ml (7 fl oz) olive oil

1. Liquidise together the pine kernels, garlic and Parmesan.

2. Add the basil and olive oil, and liquidise until smooth.

3. Decant into small clean jars with screw-on lids, and store in the fridge.

Basic 36
Creamed Parsley

This bright green sauce-garnish is used as a base for a scallop. It can be made the day before, and warmed through (very gently) at the last minute. It could also be frozen.

---

4 portions

1 bunch flat or curly parsley (we use 50/50)
2 teaspoons unsalted butter

1 shallot, finely chopped
20 ml (¾ fl oz) double cream

---

1. Pick the parsley leaves from the stalks, and blanch them for 2 minutes in boiling water.
2. You now have two options. You can drain the leaves, refresh them in cold water and drain again. Or you can drain them then, wearing rubber gloves, give them a good squeeze. This latter option keeps the colour well. Coarsely chop the leaves.
3. Melt the butter in a small pan and sweat off the shallot until softened.
4. Add the cream, and when it starts to reduce, add the parsley leaves, stirring vigorously. When all the ingredients emulsify together, the garnish is ready to use.

Basic 37
Tapenade

I often use this in fish sauces but it is also good on warm toast.

---

8 portions

250 g (9 oz) good black olives, stoned	25 g (1 oz) capers, drained
	1½ garlic cloves
50 g (2 oz) anchovies	2 tablespoons olive oil

---

1. Place all the ingredients, apart from the olive oil, in a blender. Blend for about 5 minutes, then add the oil.
2. Decant into small clean jars with screw-on lids, and store in the fridge, for up to three months.

Basic 38
Risotto Base

This basic recipe *prepares* enough rice for risotto for six. However, it is advisable to *cook* only two portions of risotto at a time. Use stock that will be appropriate to the flavour of the main ingredient.

---

6 portions

300 g (11 oz) risotto rice	200 ml (7 fl oz) white wine
3 shallots, finely chopped	600 ml (1 pint) Chicken or
100 ml (3½ fl oz) olive oil	Fish Stock (basics 1, 7)

TIP

This risotto base can be kept in the fridge for up to 4 hours before going on to the next stage – which will take about 8 minutes.

1. Sweat the shallot in the olive oil until soft, about 5 minutes. Then add the rice and sweat for a minute or so longer.
2. Deglaze with the white wine, and reduce to a syrup.
3. Add the stock, bring to the boil and simmer for 6 minutes.
4. Strain through a sieve, keeping the liquid. Leave to cool on a tray.

Basic 39
Risotto of Herbs

Good with the roast rabbit on page 79.

---

2 portions

100 g (4 oz) prepared Risotto
    Base (see above)
1 tablespoon cooking liquor
100 ml (3¹/₂ fl oz) Chicken
    Stock (basic 1)
¹/₂ tablespoon freshly grated
    Parmesan

20 g (³/₄ oz) unsalted butter
1 tablespoon freshly
    chopped chives
salt and freshly ground white
    pepper

---

1. Place the prepared rice in a saucepan, and add the cooking liquor and stock. Cook on a medium heat for about 5-6 minutes, stirring.

2. When the liquid has virtually disappeared, sprinkle in the Parmesan, then work in the butter until the rice becomes creamy and light. To finish, add the chives and season to taste with salt and pepper.

Basic 40
Risotto of Ink

Good with the baby squid on page 32.

---

2 portions

100 g (4 oz) prepared Risotto
    Base (see page 139)
1 tablespoon cooking liquor
100 ml (3¹/₂ fl oz) Fish Stock
    (basic 7)
1 sachet squid ink

¹/₂ tablespoon freshly grated
    Parmesan
1 tablespoon double cream,
    lightly whipped
salt and freshly ground white
    pepper

---

1. Place the prepared rice in a saucepan and add the cooking liquor, stock and ink. Cook on a medium heat for 4-6 minutes, stirring.

2. When the liquid has virtually disappeared, sprinkle in the Parmesan, then work in the cream to give the rice a light and fluffy texture. Season with salt and pepper.

Basic 41
Saffron Risotto

We serve this as a starter in The Canteen; it's one of the best of risottos.

2 portions

100 g (4 oz) prepared Risotto Base (see page 139)	25 g (1 oz) unsalted butter
1 tablespoon cooking liquor	50 ml (2 fl oz) whipping cream, lightly whipped
100 ml (3½ fl oz) Veal Stock (basic 3)	salt and freshly ground white pepper
a pinch of saffron strands	lemon juice
½ tablespoon freshly grated Parmesan	

1. Place the prepared rice in a saucepan, and add the cooking liquor, stock and saffron. Cook on a medium heat for 4-6 minutes, stirring.

2. When the liquid has virtually disappeared, sprinkle in the Parmesan, then work in first the butter to slightly thicken the rice, and then the cream to make it smooth and creamy.

3. Season with salt, pepper and lemon juice to taste.

Basic 42
Roast Shallots

A good garnish for meat. Make in the morning, if you like, and heat up gently to serve.

2-4 portions

8 large shallots
rock salt
2 bay leaves

1 sprig fresh thyme
300 ml (10 fl oz) olive oil

---

1. Trim the root of the shallots and take off any loose leaves of skin, leaving a perfect shape, still with the skin on.
2. Cover the bottom of a small ovenproof pan with rock salt. Place the shallots on top of the salt and add the bay leaves, thyme and the olive oil.
3. Cover with foil and cook for 3 hours in the oven preheated to 150°C/300°F/Gas 2, or until the shallots are tender.

Basic 43
Confit of Garlic

A good garnish for a number of dishes. Make in advance, a day at most.

2-4 portions

duck fat to cover the garlic
2 bay leaves
2 small sprigs fresh thyme

12-16 large garlic cloves,
     unpeeled

---

1. Half fill a small saucepan with the duck fat, and then place on the stove until the temperature reaches about 90°C/194°F.

2. Add the bay leaves, thyme and garlic. Bring the fat back to about 80°C/176°F. Cook at this temperature for about 20-30 minutes.

3. After 20 minutes, check to see if the garlic is tender to the touch. If it is, remove from the heat and allow to cool in the duck fat.

Basic 44
Pomme Fondant

You could make this about an hour in advance, which allows the potato to absorb the butter.

4 portions

4 medium potatoes	salt and freshly ground white
100 g (4 oz) unsalted butter, diced	pepper
	50 ml (2 fl oz) water

1. Peel and square off each potato. Using a 5 cm (2 in) plain round cutter cut a fondant shape out of each potato. Using a potato peeler, round off the sharp edges of each fondant.

2. Using a saucepan with a base diameter of about 15 cm (6 in), so that the fondants can sit comfortably in the bottom, line the bottom of the pan with the diced butter.

3. Place the fondant potatoes on the butter and season with salt and pepper. Pour the water on to this, and cook on a slow heat for about 15 minutes on either side until the potatoes are golden brown.

Basic 45
Pomme Purée

You can make this in advance, in the morning say, but I like to make and serve it straightaway.

---

4 portions

4 large potatoes	**100 g (4 oz) unsalted butter**
salt and freshly ground white pepper	

---

1. Peel the potatoes, place in a large saucepan and cover with cold water. Add 1 tablespoon salt, bring to the boil, and simmer until tender.
2. Drain off the potato, and place in a vegetable mill. Purée then pass through a fine sieve.
3. Beat in 75 g (3 oz) of the butter and season to taste. At this stage the purée can be kept aside in the fridge.
4. To serve, warm the purée through in a saucepan, and beat in the remaining butter. Season to taste, and serve.

Basic 46
Pomme Boulangère

A good garnish for fish dishes, or dishes with olive oil. Serve something like grilled tuna or red mullet on *top* of the boulangère.

---

4 portions

4 medium potatoes	**2 shallots, very finely chopped**
salt and freshly ground white pepper	**120 ml (4 fl oz) Fish Stock (basic 7)**
2 garlic cloves, very finely chopped	**120 ml (4 fl oz) water**

---

1. Peel and square off each potato. Using a 5 cm (2 in) plain round cutter, cut out a fondant-shaped potato. Slice finely on a mandoline producing 2 mm ($1/16$ in) thick round discs.
2. Season with salt and pepper and mix with the garlic and shallot.
3. Draw round a 7-10 cm (3-4 in) ring mould four times on to a piece of greaseproof paper. Layer the slices of potato around the inside of the lines on the paper, into approximately two layers each time so you have four potato disc shapes.
4. Place the greaseproof paper with the potato discs on it in a shallow ovenproof frying pan. Add the stock and water, and cover with the ring moulds.
5. Bring to the boil on top of the stove then place in the oven preheated to 160°C/325°F/Gas 3 for 6 minutes, or until cooked.

Basic 47
Buttered Cabbage

Cut and cook at the very last moment to keep texture, flavour and colour.

4-6 portions

1 Savoy cabbage
salt and freshly ground white
  pepper
100 g (4 oz) clarified butter

1. Cut the cabbage in half, and cut out the thick stem. Shred the leaves finely.
2. Blanch in boiling salted water for 1 minute only, then drain.
3. Heat the clarified butter in a large frying pan and toss the cabbage in this for a further minute or so. Season with salt and pepper and serve while still a little crisp.

Basic 48
Braised Cabbage

This could be made a day or so in advance. It's good with
pigeon and other game dishes.

---

4 portions

1 whole white cabbage
50 ml (2 fl oz) duck fat
1 garlic clove, finely
   chopped
½ large shallot, finely
   chopped

100 g (4 oz) smoked bacon,
   rinded and cut into fine
   strips (lardons)
200 ml (7 fl oz) Veal Stock
   (basic 3)
100 ml (3½ fl oz) Chicken
   Stock (basic 1)

---

1. Cut the cabbage into four. Remove and discard the
coarse stalk, then shred the leaves finely.
2. Heat the duck fat and fry off the garlic and shallot until
softened, then add the lardons and cook until golden brown.
3. Add the cabbage, sweating it off and making sure that
most of the natural water in the cabbage has evaporated.
4. Add the veal and chicken stocks and bring to the boil.
Cover with a lid and cook in the oven preheated to
160°C/325°F/Gas 3 for 30 minutes, or until tender.

Basic 49
Tian of Aubergine

This interesting garnish goes well with lamb or fish. The
aubergine slices, being thick, do not absorb as much oil as
thinner ones would.

---

4 portions

1 medium aubergine
olive oil
a little fresh Tomato Fondue
   (basic 34)

4 'Sun-Dried' Tomatoes,
   halved (basic 59)
flakes of sea salt (*fleur de
   sel*)

---

1. Cut the aubergine across the width into four 4 cm (1½ in) slices. Prick the flesh with a fork.

2. Shallow-fry the aubergine slices in olive oil until evenly cooked and slightly soft. Drain well on kitchen paper.

3. Cover the top of the 'tian' with tomato fondue, and then top that with two slices of sun-dried tomato. Sprinkle with *fleur de sel*.

Basic 50
Vichy Carrots

These are best cooked just before serving.

4 portions

8 large carrots	caster sugar
50 g (2 oz) unsalted butter	about 200 ml (7 fl oz) mineral
salt	water

1. Peel the carrots, and cut grooves in them lengthways using a cannelle knife. Slice very thinly on a mandoline.

2. Melt the butter in a large frying pan, and sweat off the carrot slices.

3. Add a pinch of salt and a slightly larger pinch of sugar. Continue sweating for a few more minutes.

4. Deglaze with the water (preferably Vichy, of course), and cook and reduce to a glaze.

Basic 51
Parsnip Purée

This can be made half a day in advance. Warm through carefully and thoroughly. If you like, garnish the purée with Garniture Bourgogne (basic 58).

---

4 portions

450 g (1 lb) parsnips	**salt**
1 small potato	**120 g (4½ oz) unsalted**
450 ml (15 fl oz) milk	**butter**
150 ml (5 fl oz) water	

---

1. Peel and chop the parsnips and the potato and put in a saucepan. Cover with the milk and water, and add a large pinch of salt. Cook until really soft.

2. Drain through a colander, then press down to remove excess moisture. Pass through a vegetable mill, then through a fine sieve.

3. Add 100 g (4 oz) of the butter and some salt to taste. Mix together and keep aside.

4. To serve, add the remaining butter and gently heat through. Serve immediately.

TIP

You could make a celeriac purée in much the same way. Omit the potato, use milk only, and then you can liquidise.

Basic 52
Etuvée of Endive

The vegetables should be prepared and cooked just before serving.

---

2 portions

2 large Belgian endives (chicory)
75 g (3 oz) unsalted butter, or 3 tablespoons olive oil
Chicken Stock (basic 1) to cover

salt and freshly ground white pepper
a pinch of caster sugar

---

1. Remove any discoloured outer leaves from the endives and cut off any green at the top. Cut off the root end. Divide lengthways into thirds or quarters, depending on size.
2. Put the butter or oil in a large pan and gently sweat off the endive for a few minutes without colouring.
3. Add the stock to barely cover, and continue to cook on a high heat until the stock and butter have virtually evaporated to a beautiful glaze, and the vegetables are perfectly cooked.

TIP

For an Etuvée of Leeks, use 10 baby leeks per person and cook as above.
For an Etuvée of Asparagus, use 10 small asparagus spears per person, and cook as above.
You could also have mixtures of vegetables. Cook 1 large endive with slices from a medium fennel bulb for Etuvée of Fennel and Endive; and 5 small asparagus spears with 5 baby leeks for an Etuvée of Asparagus and Leeks.

Basic 53
Confit of Fennel

Baby fennel can occasionally be found – the young 'shoots' before they swell into a bulb – or you can slice the more familiar plump bulbs instead.

4 portions

8 baby fennel 'bulbs'	12-16 olives, pitted and
salt	halved
50 ml (2 fl oz) olive oil	

1. Trim the fennel 'bulbs' 1 cm (1/2 in) from the stalks (or trim and slice 1 or 2 medium bulbs). Blanch for 3 minutes in boiling salted water then refresh in iced water. Strain and dry.
2. To serve, heat through in the olive oil with the olives until tender, about 2 minutes, depending on size.

Basic 54
Roast Salsify

To keep the white colour, the vegetable needs to be cooked in a *blanc*. This can be done some time in advance of final cooking and serving.

6 portions

450 g (1 lb) salsify	1 teaspoon white wine
900 ml (1 1/2 pints) water	vinegar
75 g (3 oz) plain flour	a little salt
juice of 1 lemon	1 tablespoon clarified butter

1. Top, tail, wash and peel the salsify. Cut into suitable lengths.
2. Mix the water, flour, lemon juice, vinegar and a little salt together in a suitable pan, and immediately immerse the prepared salsify.

3. Bring to the boil then cook gently until barely tender (depending on the thickness of the salsify). Test with the point of a sharp knife. Leave in the *blanc* to cool.

4. Drain, wash briefly, and dry. Sauté in the clarified butter at the last moment to give a little colour.

Basic 55
Ratatouille

This is a drier than normal ratatouille which is very useful as a garnish.

---

4 small portions

2 red and 2 yellow peppers	25 g (1 oz) fresh Tomato
2 large courgettes	Fondue (basic 34)
1 small aubergine	6 fresh basil leaves, cut into
1 small onion	thin strips
1 plum tomato	salt and freshly ground white
olive oil	pepper

---

1. Skin and seed the peppers, then cut them into small dice. Cut the skin and a little flesh from the courgettes and aubergine – about 5 mm (¼ in) thick – and then dice this (use the remaining flesh in another dish). Peel and cut the onion into small dice. Skin, seed and dice the tomato.

2. Heat a little olive oil in a large pan and cook the pepper dice gently for a few minutes. They should still be crisp and bright in colour. Remove with a slotted spoon to a plate.

3. Cook the courgette, aubergine and onion dice separately in the same pan, using a little more olive oil each time, so that they too remain bright and crisp. Remove with a slotted spoon to a plate.

4. Heat the tomato fondue gently in a thick-based pan, add the basil and cook for 1 minute.

5. Add all the vegetable dice to this, including the tomato, and gently mix together over gentle heat. Season.

Basic 56
Beignets of Sage

Prepare the tapenade well in advance, and the batter 3 hours before using. Fry the beignets at the last moment.

4 portions

at least 16 large fresh
  sage leaves
1 tablespoon Tapenade
  (basic 37)
olive oil for shallow-
  frying

Batter
25 g (1 oz) fresh yeast
250 ml (8 fl oz) beer
  (we use Belgian lager,
  which makes for a very
  light batter)
200 g (7 oz) plain flour, sieved
a pinch of salt

1. For the batter, dissolve the yeast in a little of the beer which has been warmed gently on the stove to blood temperature. Then incorporate the rest of the beer.

2. Place the flour in a bowl and make a well in the centre. Slowly pour in the beer and yeast mixture, whisking continuously until all has been incorporated. The batter should be quite runny. Stand for about 3 hours to allow it to activate.

3. Sandwich two sage leaves together with a little of the tapenade. Make eight 'sandwiches', two per portion.

4. Heat the olive oil in a pan. Dip the sage leaves in the batter and then shallow-fry in the hot oil until light and crisp.

TIP

A good garnish for red mullet and any grilled fish. It could also be served as a canapé. The batter can also be used to coat deep-fried salsify, green beans or other vegetables.

Basic 57
Mushroom Ravioli

These are delicious as a garnish for pigeon (see page 77), but can of course be served as a pasta dish. The chicken mousse can be cooked as a savoury mousse by itself.

---

4 portions

200 g (7 oz) chanterelles or other wild mushrooms, chopped
4 shallots, chopped
4 garlic cloves, chopped
25 g (1 oz) unsalted butter
80 g (3¼ oz) cooked spinach
100 g (4 oz) Fresh Pasta (basic 65)

Chicken mousse
100 g (4 oz) chicken breast, skinned
salt and freshly ground white pepper
a pinch of ground mace
½ egg white
150 ml (5 fl oz) double cream

---

1. Sweat the mushrooms, shallots and garlic in the butter until softened. Allow to cool, then roughly chop. Chop the spinach as well, and mix into the mushrooms.
2. Make the chicken mousse. Cut the chicken into suitably sized pieces and place in the food processor. Season with salt, pepper and mace, and purée thoroughly. Cool a little before adding the egg white and cream. Pulse briefly, just to mix. Pass through a fine sieve, then chill if not using straightaway.
3. Bind the mushroom and spinach mixture with the chicken mousse.
4. Roll out the fresh pasta, and cut into four large circles. Place the filling on one half, and fold the other half over, sticking the edges firmly together with water, to make a half-moon shape. Trim if necessary.
5. Make sure the filling is securely contained, then poach in boiling salted water for 4 minutes. Drain well and serve.

Basic 58
Garniture Bourgogne

All three elements of the garnish can be prepared in advance. The onions keep extremely well in the stock, which will set to a jelly.

---

4 portions

200 g (7 oz) small button mushrooms
20 g (¾ oz) unsalted butter
salt and freshly ground white pepper
200 g (7 oz) smoked bacon, rinded and cut into thin lardons

a little vegetable oil
200 g (7 oz) silverskin onions, peeled
Veal Stock to cover (basic 3)

---

1. Sweat the mushrooms until tender in the butter. Drain well and season.
2. Cook the bacon lardons in oil in a non-stick pan until crisp. Drain.
3. Cook the onions in the veal stock until soft, then leave in the stock.
4. Heat each up individually, and drain off. Sprinkle over the top of each individual portion.

> **TIP**
>
> *This is the traditional accompaniment to a daube of beef, scattered over each portion as it is served. It is also a welcome addition to a parsnip purée (basic 51), adding flavour and texture.*

Basic 59
'Sun-Dried' Tomatoes

These tomatoes are not desiccated but softish, tangy and well flavoured. You must use plum tomatoes.

---

1 kg (2¹/₄ lb) plum tomatoes
rock salt
olive oil

fresh thyme leaves
garlic cloves, peeled and
   sliced

---

1. Skin, halve and seed the tomatoes, then place on a baking tray, 'cup' up.
2. Sprinkle with salt, oil, thyme and garlic slices to taste.
3. Put in the oven preheated to the lowest possible heat, and leave to dry for 10 hours. Keep in an airtight jar, in olive oil.

Basic 60
Foie Gras Butter

This makes a very special tasting butter which is used mainly in Sauce Albufera (basic 13), an accompaniment to poultry, or in a sauce for ravioli (see page 33). Keep refrigerated for up to a week, or freeze in little blocks.

Makes 150 g (5 oz)

75 g (3 oz) cooked foie gras   **75 g (3 oz) unsalted butter**

---

1. Have the foie gras and butter at room temperature so they have the same consistency.
2. Either put both into a food processor, blend together, and then push through a fine sieve, or sieve the foie gras on its own and then whisk in the butter.
3. Form into a suitable shape or shapes, and chill or freeze.

> **TIP**
>
> *You can make this butter with raw foie gras, but the proportions have to change: use 100 g (4 oz) foie gras to 50 g (2 oz) butter.*

Basic 61
Garlic Butter

This is the butter to serve with grilled lobster (see page 51) but it would also be ideal for snails.

1-2 portions

200 g (7 oz) unsalted butter, softened

50 g (2 oz) shallots, very finely chopped

100 g (4 oz) fresh parsley, very finely chopped

10 g (¼ oz) puréed garlic

120 ml (4 fl oz) Pernod

1. Mix all the ingredients together.
2. Chill until ready to use. It will last for two days or so, or it can be frozen.

Basic 62
Soft Herb Crust

A good topping for fish. Use white breadcrumbs, preferably brioche.

8 portions

175 g (6 oz) fresh bread-crumbs

80 g (3¼ oz) Gruyère cheese, grated

50 g (2 oz) fresh parsley, chopped

5 g (⅛ oz) fresh thyme, chopped

125 g (4½ oz) unsalted butter, softened

salt and freshly ground white pepper

1. Place all the ingredients in a food processor and process until thoroughly mixed.
2. Spread out on to a greaseproof-paper-lined tray and open-freeze. Package in quantities suitable for later use, and return to the freezer.

Basic 63
Mouginoise

This makes a delicious topping for turbot (see pages 46–7), and it can be made a day in advance. In The Restaurant, we make it from trimmings of salmon, foie gras and chicken.

about 10 portions

100 g (4 oz) skinned and boned salmon fillet
100 g (4 oz) foie gras
100 g (4 oz) skinned and boned chicken breast
½ slice of white bread
½ egg white
350 ml (12 fl oz) double cream

25 g (1 oz) unsalted butter
10 g (¼ oz) finely diced shallot
250 g (9 oz) girolles, sliced thinly
1 small black truffle, sliced

1. In a blender, blend the salmon, foie gras and chicken breast together to a purée.
2. Add the white bread, egg white and cream, and blend together again.
3. In a small frying pan melt the butter and sauté the shallot and girolles until softened, but without colouring. Leave to cool.
4. When cold, fold the girolles and shallots into the blended mixture along with the sliced truffle.

Basic 64
Mushroom Duxelles

Make in advance and use as a garnish for Cod Viennoise (see page 58).

Makes about 50 g (2 oz)

225 g (8 oz) cultivated
   mushrooms
salt and freshly ground white
   pepper

1 tablespoon whipping
   cream

---

1. Wipe the mushrooms and trim the stalks if necessary. Chop very finely in a processor or by hand.
2. Heat in a dry pan until their liquid comes out and evaporates, and the mushrooms shrink.
3. Add the cream and mix in to bind the mushrooms.

Basic 65
Fresh Pasta

This can be made in advance and frozen.

Makes 600 g (1¼ lb)

600 g (1¼ lb) plain white
   flour
4 eggs

6 egg yolks
2 tablespoons olive oil
a pinch of salt

---

1. Place the flour in a food processor, and switch the machine on.
2. Slowly add the eggs and egg yolks, using the pulse button.
3. When all the egg has been amalgamated, add the olive oil and salt and mix in briefly.
4. Remove from the machine and knead for a few minutes on a lightly floured surface. Cover with cling film and allow to rest for at least an hour before rolling and cutting as appropriate.

Basic 66
Puff Pastry

This pastry will keep for a day or two in the fridge, and it also freezes well.

Makes about 1.1 kg (2½ lb)

450 g (1 lb) strong plain
   flour, sieved
1 teaspoon salt
450 g (1 lb) unsalted butter,
   softened slightly

180 ml (6½ fl oz) water
2 teaspoons white wine
   vinegar

---

1. Sieve the flour into a circle on your work surface. Make a well in the middle and put into this the salt, 60 g (2¼ oz) of the butter, the water and the vinegar. Mix and knead until the dough is smooth and elastic. Mould the dough into a ball and score a cross with a knife across the top. Cover the dough with a cloth and leave to rest in a cool place for about an hour.

2. On a lightly floured surface, roll the dough into a sheet about 20 cm (8 in) square, rolling the corners (the tails of the cross) a little more thinly than the centre.

3. Place the remaining butter in a block in the centre of the dough. Bring up the four corners of pastry over the butter to make an envelope.

4. Roll this out into a rectangle about 25 x 15 cm (10 x 6 in) and fold in three. Turn this folded rectangle by 90 degrees. This constitutes a 'turn'.

5. Ensuring the rolling pin is at right angles to the folds, roll out again to a rectangle the same size as before, and fold in three again as before. Again turn the pastry by 90 degrees (in the same direction as before). Two 'turns' have now been completed.

6. Cover the dough and rest in the fridge for an hour.

7. Roll out again twice in a rectangle, fold and turn as in steps 4 and 5. Four 'turns' have now been completed. Rest the dough again in the fridge for another hour.

8. Repeat stages 4 and 5 again. Six 'turns' have now been completed. Rest the dough for one more hour in the fridge, and the dough is ready for use.

Basic 67
Poaching Syrup

This syrup is used mainly for poaching fruits, or poured *over* fruits, and can be flavoured in a variety of ways. The quantity of sugar used will depend on the sweetness of the fruit. It keeps indefinitely.

Makes about 2 litres (3½ pints)

1 litre (1¾ pints) water
700-800 g (1½-1¾ lb) caster
  sugar

relevant liqueur and/or
  flavouring (optional, see
  individual recipes)

---

1. Bring the water and sugar slowly to the boil together in a large pan. Make sure the sugar dissolves.
2. The syrup can be flavoured with vanilla or other spices such as cinnamon, and with a variety of liqueurs or alcohols – roughly 100 ml (3½ fl oz) for the above quantity of syrup.

Basic 68
Raspberry Coulis

This simple but delicious dessert sauce can be made a day or so in advance. It can also be frozen.

---

4 portions

225 g (8 oz) fresh raspberries   75 g (3 oz) icing sugar

---

1. Place the raspberries in a bowl and cover with the sugar. Leave for a while for the sugar to begin pulling out the fruit juices.
2. Purée the mixture, then pass through a fine sieve to catch all the seeds. Chill.

Basic 69
Crème Anglaise

This can be made the day before, but cover the surface with cling film so that a skin does not form.

about 10 portions

6 egg yolks
120 g (4¹/₂ oz) caster sugar

500 ml (17 fl oz) milk

1. Mix the egg yolks and sugar well together in a rounded bowl.
2. Bring the milk to the boil and pour over the eggs and sugar mixture. Mix in well, then return to the pan and to the heat.
3. Cook very slowly, stirring, until the mixture thickens enough to coat the back of your spoon.
4. Remove from the heat and pass through a fine sieve. Leave to get cold.

TIP

Various flavourings to taste can be added to this basic crème anglaise or custard. Armagnac is good, for instance, going well with the soufflé and the tarts on pages 93 and 102–3: add to taste. We occasionally add an extra egg yolk to the basic mix if additional flavouring liquid is to be used. A spice such as vanilla or cinnamon could be infused with the milk.
Never use a whisk when making crème anglaise or custard. This adds air, and you end up with a bubbly sauce. Just use a spoon.

Basic 70
Caramel Sauce

Wonderful with the apple tart on page 97, or just vanilla ice cream! Make a couple of days in advance if you like.

---

10 portions

120 g (4½ oz) caster sugar   250 ml (8 fl oz) double cream

---

1. Melt the sugar gently in a heavy-based pan, then cook to a dark caramel.
2. Add the cream – carefully, as the hot caramel will make it boil and spit – and stir together to a sauce consistency.

Basic 71
Sweet Sabayon

This delicious sauce must be made just before serving. Choose an alcohol to complement the dish the sauce is to accompany – Calvados for an apple dish, Kirsch for a cherry or other red fruit dish.

---

4 portions

2 egg yolks
200 ml (7 fl oz) syrup
  (made from 100 g/3½ oz
  caster sugar and 100 ml/
  3½ fl oz water)

100 ml (3½ oz) alcohol of
  choice

---

1. Place the egg yolks, syrup and alcohol in a wide, shallow pan, and whisk together.
2. Over a very gentle heat, continue to whisk until a foam starts to form.

3. Continue cooking very gently, whisking all the time, for at least 15 minutes, until the sabayon is cooked, light and fluffy.

Basic 72
Crème Pâtissière

This is useful as a soufflé or sweet sauce base, but it could also be used as a filling for a tart or tartlet case. Make a day in advance.

10-15 portions

6 egg yolks
75 g (3 oz) caster sugar
50 g (2 oz) plain flour
400 ml (14 fl oz) milk

100 ml (3½ fl oz) lemon juice
finely grated zest of 2
    lemons

---

1. In a pan, cream the egg yolks and sugar together well, then mix in the flour.
2. Bring the milk, lemon juice and zest to the boil in another pan, then pour a little into the egg yolk pan, whisking until smooth.
3. Add the remainder of the liquid, and cook over a gentle heat, stirring, to a smooth cream, for no longer than 5 minutes.

Basic 73
Vanilla Ice Cream

Make a couple of days in advance. Very good with the apple tart on page 97.

---

10 portions

6 egg yolks	6 vanilla pods, split, or
120 g (4½ oz) caster sugar	vanilla essence to taste
500 ml (17 fl oz) milk	200 ml (7 fl oz) double cream

---

1. Mix the egg yolks and sugar together well in a rounded bowl.

2. Put the milk and the vanilla pods and scraped-out seeds in a pan and bring to the boil.

3. Pour the hot liquid over the yolk mixture and mix well.

4. Return the mixture to the pan and to the heat, and cook very slowly, stirring, until the mixture thickens enough to coat the back of your spoon. This, basically, is a highly flavoured crème anglaise.

5. Remove from the heat and pass through a fine sieve into a bowl over ice to cool it down quickly.

6. When cold, whip in the whipped cream. Put in an ice-cream machine and churn until frozen, or freeze in the freezer.

Basic 74
Apricot Purée

This can be used as a sauce, either as it is or to thicken up a juice such as orange.

1. Use the same amount of apricots and syrup as for Poached Apricots (below), but cook the apricots until really tender.
2. Drain, keeping the syrup, and remove the vanilla pods. Liquidise the apricots and vanilla seeds, and pass through a sieve.
3. The purée will be quite thick, studded with the black of the vanilla seeds. You can thin it down, if wanted, with a little of the syrup (or with some fruit juice).

Basic 75
Poached Apricots

Serve these with the soufflé on page 92, or in a poached fruit dish (see pages 88–9). Keep for a couple of days in the fridge.

---

4 portions

900 g (2 lb) fresh apricots	**Cointreau**
Poaching Syrup to cover (basic 67)	**2 vanilla pods**

---

1. Halve and stone the apricots, and place in a small pan. Cover with syrup, and add the Cointreau (50 ml/2 fl oz per 500 ml/17 fl oz syrup). Split the vanilla pods, scrape the seeds into the pan, and add the pods as well.
2. Bring up to the boil, then remove from the heat immediately. Leave the apricots to cool in the syrup. They will be firm and delicious.

Basic 76
Marinated Prunes

You can actually make this in any quantity you desire. The prunes last well, for up to three months or so, and can be useful in a variety of ways – in the tarts on pages 102–3 and the soufflé on page 93. They could also be made into an ice cream.

1 kg (2¹/₄ lb) good prunes, pitted	syrup made from 120 ml (4 fl oz) water and 120 g (4¹/₂ oz) caster sugar
about 250 ml (8 fl oz) dark rum	
about 250 ml (8 fl oz) Armagnac	

1. Place the pitted prunes in a suitable container – a preserving or Kilner jar or jars would be perfect.
2. Cover with the rum, Armagnac and syrup.
3. Cover with the lid and leave in the fridge to marinate for at least two weeks before use.

Basic 77
Prune and Armagnac Soufflé Base

This quantity of soufflé base will serve up to twenty portions. Freeze it in the portions which will be most useful to you. Per person you need a good dessertspoon, but you would rarely make a soufflé for one, so portions of 4 dessertspoons might be more handy.

20 portions

500 g (18 oz) Marinated Prunes (basic 76)	100 ml (3¹/₂ fl oz) Armagnac
30 g (1¹/₄ oz) cornflour	100 g (4 oz) caster sugar
	50 ml (2 fl oz) water

1. Make sure all the prune stones are removed, then blend the prunes in a processor. Pass through a fine sieve into a saucepan. Bring to the boil, then simmer, stirring.

2. Dissolve the cornflour in the Armagnac, and add this to the prunes. Stir and cook vigorously until it thickens, then cook for a few minutes more. Remove from the heat.

3. Mix the sugar and water together in a separate pan and boil up to 121°C (250°F). Add to the prune mixture and mix in well.

4. Leave to cool, then freeze (see page 166).

Basic 78
Sweet Pastry

This is the pastry to use for sweet tarts (see pages 101–3). You will need roughly half this quantity – 500 g (18 oz) – per tart. It freezes well, but do wrap carefully.

Makes 1 kg (2¹/₄ lb)

700 g (1¹/₂ lb) unsalted butter	100 ml (3¹/₂ fl oz) water
300 g (11 oz) icing sugar	1 kg (2¹/₄ lb) plain flour
8 egg yolks	

---

1. Cream the butter and sugar together in an electric mixer bowl until soft and white.

2. Add the egg yolks and beat in thoroughly. Turn the machine off, remove the lid, and scrape the sides down into the mixture to make sure everything is incorporated. Blend again.

3. Add a little of the water, then add the flour, and mix together thoroughly. Stop the machine every now and again and scrape the sides into the bulk of the mixture.

4. Add the remaining water and mix for 2-3 minutes.

5. Remove, wrap in cling film and chill for at least 1 hour before using.

ACKNOWLEDGEMENTS

I should like to thank the following:

Tony Allen of Cutty Catering for the support he has given me over the last eight years, both as a friend and in business; Mr Chiandetti of Forte, who made my venture at the Hyde Park Hotel possible, and who has continued to support me; Michael Caine, for his faith in me, and for his friendship; Claudio Pulze, for being at my side for many years, and for being a godfather to my son; Eugene McCoy, Tony Zivanarez and David Coverdale, for being outrageous and making me laugh; Keith Floyd, Albert Roux and Michael Winner for the stories they have told me (and the lies!); Keith Skeal for his trust and support in the early days when I'd run out of money; Nigel Platts-Martin and Richard Carr for their support in Harvey's; Susan Fleming and Roger Pizey, without whom this book would not have been possible.